I0521058

Marie's Awakening

The Next Chapter: A Journey from Healing to Wholeness

Marie's Awakening

The Next Chapter: A Journey from Healing to Wholeness

A deeply personal, faith-driven testimony of one woman's walk through betrayal, loss, abuse, and pain—and the redemptive power of God's grace that met her there. With raw honesty and spiritual insight, Yvonne Rimmer shares how healing is just the beginning—and wholeness is the victory. This is a story of surrender, of rising again, and of becoming a vessel of hope for others still in the fight.

Yvonne Rimmer

Marie's Awakening

The Next Chapter: A Journey from Healing to Wholeness

© 2026 Yvonne Rimmer
All rights reserved.

No part of this publication may be reproduced, stored in a retrieval system, or transmitted in any form or by any means—electronic, mechanical, photocopy, recording, or otherwise—without prior written permission of the publisher, except for brief quotations used in reviews or scholarly works.

Scripture quotations taken from the Holy Bible, New International Version®, NIV®. Copyright ©1973, 1978, 1984, 2011 by Biblica, Inc.™ Used by permission. All rights reserved worldwide.

This book is a work of nonfiction based on the author's personal experiences and reflections. Any names, events, or details have been presented truthfully to the best of the author's ability.

GHW
MINISTRIES

www.godshandywork.org

ISBN: 979-8-9988502-1-9
Published by God's Handywork, Inc.
Murfreesboro, Tennessee
Printed in the United States of America

Library of Congress Control Number: 2025927800

Dedication

First, to the Lord of my life—Jesus Christ, my Savior, my refuge, my guiding light. You are the One who whispered hope into my weary soul and breathed life into my story when I thought all was lost—this book is for You. Your healing hand has restored me, Your unfailing love has sustained me, and Your divine direction has led me through the valleys into the promise of new beginnings. Without You, I am nothing; but in You, I have found strength, purpose, and a love beyond measure. You are faithful in every season, constant in every storm, and gracious beyond understanding.

May this work be a testimony to Your goodness, a reflection of Your mercy, and an offering of gratitude for the endless ways You have moved in my life.

Second, to my family:

To my beloved husband, Timothy—a man of unwavering faith, steadfast love, and immeasurable strength. Your godly wisdom, support, and devotion have been my guiding light, lifting me through every challenge and celebrating every triumph. This book is a reflection of all that you and God have inspired in me—thank you for walking this journey with me, hand in hand, heart to heart. I am forever grateful for the blessing you are.

And to my children, who are the world to me and have been my inspiration for so many days: You are stronger than you realize and are overcomers. You were designed with purpose and are important to the Kingdom of God. Make Jesus proud. I love you!

Third, to the one who struggles yet refuses to be defeated— To the courageous soul who presses on, fighting the good fight of faith even when the road is steep and the burdens heavy—this book is for you. May its words be a sanctuary in your storm, a whisper of encouragement when silence feels deafening, and a light illuminating the path ahead when the way seems unclear.

You are a testament to resilience, a warrior clothed in grace, and a beacon of unwavering hope. Through every trial and triumph, may you find renewed strength to endure—knowing that perseverance births victory and faith carries you beyond the impossible.

You are not alone, and this journey—though difficult—is refining you, shaping you, and leading you toward the glorious finish. Hold fast, dear fighter. Press onward. The reward is nearer than you know.

Fourth, to the person who finds the strength to Be the One—May your heart be an unwavering flame of hope, your words a soothing balm to the weary, and your presence a guiding light to those who are lost.

You're called to Be the One—to reach, to minister, and to walk alongside others on their healing journey. Your kindness is a bridge, your wisdom a refuge, and your love a testimony of grace. Never underestimate the ripple effect of your compassion; through you, broken spirits will find restoration, wounded souls will rediscover strength, and hearts yearning for truth will be filled with renewed purpose. You are chosen. You are equipped. You are meant to Be the One.

Preface

Healing is a yearning whispered in the hearts of many, yet its purpose often remains a mystery. It's not merely the mending of wounds, but the first step on a sacred journey—a journey into the depths of God's divine plan, far beyond what human understanding can grasp. As *Isaiah* declares,

> *"For my thoughts are not your thoughts, neither are your ways my ways," declares the Lord.—Isaiah 55:8 NIV*

We were never meant to be imprisoned by the ghosts of our past—by torment, pain, or failures that threaten to define us. Jesus longs for us to live whole, not just to exist, but to thrive—immersed in joy, purpose, and the boundless love He offers.

Healing is more than personal restoration; it's a beacon that reaches beyond self. Whether we seek renewal within or are ready to extend a hand to another, every wound we endure carries a divine purpose. In the depths of suffering, something sacred stirs—a refining fire that births strength, peace, and an unshakable love, weaving together a life of enduring joy. It's not the Lord's will for you to suffer in silence. *Now* is the time to rise, to embrace all that you have endured, and to turn it into a testimony of His glory.

For years, I wrestled with the chains of an abusive past—shadows that clung to me, whispering lies of brokenness and unworthiness. Yet amid my deepest despair, I found purpose. *Then God.* In His unfathomable mercy, doors I never dreamed, opened before me, and opportunities for ministry—ones I felt painfully inadequate for—began to take shape. Yet I've learned that God doesn't just call those who are already whole, already polished, already prepared. No, more importantly, He calls the willing. He seeks vessels, not perfection—hearts willing to whisper, *"Lord, use me"*. For in His hands, the most shattered soul becomes the most radiant testimony.

I know others hear the same call—those standing at the edge of hope, wondering if light can truly pierce the depths of their sorrow. Somewhere in the unseen places, a voice cries out, pleading for a way forward, for proof that redemption is possible. This is a continuous of my story, but I pray, Dear Reader, that it may mark the beginning of yours.

Table of Contents

One: Awakened By Grace

The Moment That Changed Everything

I t all happened in an instant—an extraordinary moment unlike any I had ever known. God's healing hand reached down from Heaven and awakened me from the depths of despair, wrapping His virtue around my wounded, aching heart. I buried my face in the floor as tears pooled beneath me—tears of release, of relief. Why hadn't I found healing sooner? Why had it been so difficult to relinquish the pain? Up until this point, I had experienced wave after wave of frustration. But in that moment, I felt His embrace and knew—for the first time—that life was going to be different. I never imagined how profoundly everything was about to change—for the good of God. It began a journey that would leave me crying, laughing, struggling, and yes, at times, confused. But oh, what a journey of Awakening, One that would forever alter my life.

As a child, I endured abuse—physical, emotional, and sexual—at the hands of a stepfather and others. The wounds burrowed deep, gnawing at my soul and slowly destroying the life I had left. It felt hopeless—until the night I felt the touch of God. I knew I had experienced miraculous healing. It felt like the final chapter had been written. But what I didn't realize was that my life was only beginning. God doesn't heal just to leave—He heals to redeem. His desire is to use our struggle for good. I felt changed. I was changed. My life was about to reveal the hand of God at work—a transformation unfolding in ways I never expected. I was in unfamiliar territory. The joy was unspeakable. The pain lifted—if only for a moment. I knew I had been healed. But what I didn't realize was... there was more. God wasn't finished.

Was I ready for the adventure ahead? Did I have the courage, the strength, and the determination to press forward? God knew my heart was ready. He met me at the center of my sorrow and gently began to wipe away my tears. I felt His healing touch—His virtue soothing every fear and calming every doubt. I buried my face in His embrace. It was in that moment that my journey to "Wholeness" truly began. I experienced overwhelming joy and peace. I praised God, fully convinced that my life would never be the same. And it hasn't been—though not always in the ways I expected. God's ways are far above ours.

My hope is that within the pages of this book, God will bring clarity—a clarity that offers direction, promotes understanding, and opens hearts to His purpose. God designed healing not as the end of the road, but as the beginning. A beginning through which lives can be forever changed—as we go "From Healing to Wholeness." But do we truly understand wholeness? To become whole is more than just being healed. It's when our mind and heart return to their intended purpose: to love, to live, and to minister—by the grace of God. Too often, we fail to recognize the value in our pain—the purpose behind the struggle. We let our emotions run unbridled. We get swept up in the rollercoaster of daily life. And if we're not careful, that pain begins to consume us—mentally, physically, and emotionally. But even in the midst of our pain, we can find peace—if we seek the heart of the Apostle Paul and declare:

"I am not saying this because I am in need, for I have learned to be content whatever the circumstances. I know what it is to be in need, and I know what it is to have plenty. I have learned the secret of being content in any and every situation, whether well fed or hungry, whether living in plenty or in want. I can do all this through him who gives me strength."— Philippians 4:11–13, NIV

Are you ready to look deep within your life? To challenge your thinking—and discover the hidden value within your pain? It's time to be honest. And through that honesty, you'll find the amazing journey of God's grace—His mercy and direction bringing meaning to all you've endured. God's desire for you is

3

wholeness. The questions stirring in your heart must be answered. Are you willing to let someone inside your walls— walls you've built to keep the enemy at bay? Walls that became a comfort zone. A place of retreat. A false protection that ended up shutting out not only the pain, but God... and the people who truly love you.

What is love—and just who is this God? You've read about Him. You've heard about Him. You've even felt Him at times. But lingering deep within your heart, one question still haunts you: Who is this God of love? You've questioned love itself— because so far, the only love you've known is the kind that wounds. An abusive, confusing, distorted version of love. A worldly love that has left you broken. Your experience of love has been perverted, tainted, and twisted. But what you may not realize is this: That's not love. It's a counterfeit. A deception from the enemy of lies—Satan himself. Because of shame, failures, and humiliation, it feels easier to hide, to disappear into yourself. Lost in what has become a shell of a life.

Longing, yearning—even aching to the very marrow of your bones—you silently cry, "Does anyone see me? Does anyone hear me? Does anyone love me?" Deep within, you know God loves you. Yet there's still a fear of letting your cries be heard. A predator—the enemy's number one lieutenant—is always listening, waiting for the moment to strike and seal your defenses. Weary and worn, you begin to doubt whether you have the strength to fight back against the relentless attack. You realize that remaining silent is nothing less than a death sentence.

Each day, a little more of your heart feels as if it's dying... and the grave begins to whisper your name. But amid this desolation, a faint ray of hope struggles to surface—a stubborn spark of defiance, refusing to be extinguished by the voice proclaiming there is no hope. You felt the touch of God—a touch that left you desiring more, needing more. And it left you wondering: Is this true love that brings healing? Is it the love I've longed for, dreamed of, and imagined? Though past hurts and lingering pain rise to silence the questions, deep in your heart, you know you must reach out one last time. And so, the quiet battle within gives you the strength to declare, "Enough is enough." You sense it's time to put the adversary on defense—because you're tired of always having to defend.

I know the price of your reach. I know the fear buried deep within your heart. I know the uncertainty and terror that revelation can spark. I recognize the value of your pain. But do you see it? Can you recognize the significance of what you've endured? How would you know sweetness without first tasting bitterness? How would you recognize healing without first feeling broken? How would you know peace without the storm? How would you find courage without fear? How could you truly experience joy without sorrow? And how would you know love—real love—without first encountering hate?

You stand at the door of indecision—and God speaks,

...then choose for yourselves this day whom you will serve...—Joshua 24:15, NIV

5

It's time to admit the truth—you've become a slave to your pain, your fears, and your past. Now the choice is yours. What will you do with the bondage of your heart? Will you walk out of the furnace of affliction by trusting God? Or will you allow the chains of your past to bind you once more? It's hard to see clearly through the curtain of tears that shrouds your heart. But God is working—just as He did in Paul's life—for your good. If you trust Him, He will open your understanding. You will see... as He envisions. If you trust Him, He will open your understanding.

"My ways and thoughts," says the Lord, "are higher than yours." Are you burdened with pride? Do you look to yourself instead of your Creator? Have doubt and unbelief made you impatient with the process? It's time to take a step back and consider the life God has designed. Can you appreciate His plan? Can you see the majesty and glory in what He does? God's timing cannot be rushed, and His plan cannot be foiled. As you trust Him—as you align your timing with His, and your will with His—you will find direction. You'll learn to rest in the certainty of His higher ways and deeper thoughts. God's Word does not return void. He will accomplish what He purposes. You can trust Him.

"As the heavens are higher than the earth, so are my ways higher than your ways and my thoughts than your thoughts."
Isaiah 55:9 NIV

There is value in the struggle—a value that, one day, will allow you to reach to another and become the vessel God saw within.

Pain can leave us struggling—physically, mentally, financially, and spiritually. In its wake, it brings confusion, exhaustion, and feelings of worthlessness. In such difficult places, it often seems impossible to find meaning. We are plagued by haunting questions—none more tormenting than this one: "Why, Lord?" We begin to interrogate God. Why did we have to endure such battles? Why the heartache, the loss, the trauma? Why a life that has left us angry, numb, and misplaced? And that is where the real battle begins. It becomes an all-out assault from the enemy, who wages war on our minds— desperately trying to distract us from the truth of what God has in store.

Our first question should not be, "Why, Lord?" It should be, "How?" To understand the how, we must turn to the Word of God—just as Jesus did when the enemy came against Him. We cannot allow the adversary to torment us with lies. We must fight back with truth. The Word declares:

"And we know that in all things God works for the good of those who love him, who have been called according to his purpose." Romans 8:28 NIV

Could it be that there's purpose in all we've suffered and endured? The answer is both humbling and empowering: Yes! It's been in front of us all along. So the real question becomes:

When will we let God turn our healing into wholeness? Because wholeness doesn't erase our struggles—it embraces them, transforming pain into purpose and wounds into a testimony. A testimony that fosters growth, healing, and strength—not only for us, but for God's glory. And when we finally step outside of yourselves—beyond the borders of our own world—we discover that God can indeed use us.

Too often, we treat healing as the end of the journey—when really, it's only the beginning. Burdened by feelings of inadequacy, brokenness, and shame, we let our pain reshape how we see ourselves. We see only the wounded, abandoned version of who we used to be. We shut out every voice—including God's. But still, He whispers: "You are somebody to Me. I can use you." That's been His intent all along. Healing isn't the destination—it's the seed. A seed that cracks open, pushes through hardened ground, and reaches toward the light. And in that process, we become what God always envisioned: a vessel of purpose. A vessel that understands pain, hardship, and struggle—and has learned to rise because of them. We stop resisting the process. We begin to embrace it. And in doing so, we see what the enemy meant for destruction, God is already using for good. The test becomes the testimony. And we become vessels—of healing, of strength, of love.

Understand this: It's only through the fire that we truly learn. Through the trials, the refining, the breaking—and yet, the strengthening. We've felt the depths of pain, carried the weight of struggle, and walked through valleys of sorrow. But we didn't stay there. We emerged—not only knowing suffering but understanding resilience. And now, another voice rises—a cry in the darkness, a plea for help. Who will see? Who will hear? Who will answer?

Will we allow our healing to remain surface-deep, or will we push beyond—stretching it into places we never imagined, into lives we never dreamed we could touch? Can we surrender our comfort, extend our reach, and minister as God calls? Who will be the one? Who will step forward? Can we pray, *"Lord Jesus, let that one be me"?*

For it's in that moment—when healing is no longer about us but becomes an offering—that we step into something greater. That, my friend, is when healing becomes *wholeness*.

Let's not get ahead of the story. These truths didn't come easily. They were forged over years—through mistakes, trials, and the struggle to find my way in life. Healing isn't a magic wand that changes everything overnight. It's a process. A daily walk that grows stronger as we learn to trust God rather than ourselves. We're human. We tend to focus on our flaws—wondering what hope remains. I'll let you in on a secret: if someone had told me I'd be where I am today... I would've laughed out loud. You see, my healing was only the launching point for a much bigger journey—a voyage across the sea of life. And once it began, my vessel faced many turbulent storms, shipwrecks, and uncertain paths. I was tossed to and fro by the angry waves of life. But God. Through the depths of struggle,

I've learned what it means to walk on water—keeping my eyes on Jesus. Yes, there were days when I doubted and began to sink. But by His grace, Jesus reached out, took my hand... and we began again.

It's okay to sink at times or make mistakes. The problem isn't the struggle—the problem is giving up. We are well able to overcome if we trust that God has a plan for our lives. The answer isn't praying for an easier journey—it's praying for strength and endurance to finish the race. I can attest, it will be enlightening and worth every step. It's a journey that will take you to heights you never knew you could reach—heights you never imagined were within you. You must remember: God's ways are higher. Don't limit God by failing to realize your full potential. He wants more for you. Don't doubt or fight the process—trust and go forth in Him.

Whether you've struggled with abuse, have been the abuser, or are simply trying to recognize both sides of the struggle—it's important to understand the wide range of emotions you may experience. Without a full understanding of God's healing, you may find yourself angry, frustrated, or irritated. What if I told you there might come a day when you'd be willing to go through everything you've experienced in life again? That might shock some. But can you see the value of your struggle? Someone who has experienced pain is better equipped to understand it. If you knew your testimony could stop a suicide... reach the brokenhearted... or minister to the deeper places in someone's soul—would you be willing to endure the hardships of life? Why would you desire to be anything less than who you are—who God created you to be? Can you push past your pain and see the bigger plan? Can you see through the eyes of God and realize you have purpose?

Now to the revelation God wants us to grasp. We tend to look at our scars and see ugliness—but what if we're looking at them the wrong way? Our scars can become trophies— reminders of battles we've survived. Evidence that Jesus heals and redeems. When Jesus revealed His scars to the disciples, He wasn't asking for pity. He was identifying Himself. He had endured the greatest trial of His life. And it didn't destroy Him— it fulfilled a divine plan that time would reveal. Your scars tell a story. Don't hide them. Thank Him for every one of them— every painful moment that gave you the chance to see His power at work. Because of Calvary—because of one selfless act—we have hope. Hope that our scars can speak. Hope that tragedy can become treasure. And that treasure? That's your testimony. The value of that testimony leads us here.

You see, my first book, Marie's Journey, was only the beginning. The story continues—just as the ministry God intended continues. Let's get to it—there are ministries and testimonies waiting to be birthed.

Two: The Walls

The Journey Beyond Yesterday

I never fully grasped the magnitude of the Healing that took place the night of the conference. In that moment, I believed it was the dawn of perfection—a new beginning where pain would cease and every burden would lift. I walked away convinced that from that day forward, life would unfold effortlessly, like a beautifully scripted story penned by divine hands. But looking back, I see now how naive my understanding was. I was young in the Lord, still learning His ways, still discovering the depths of His purpose in my life. I thought healing was the finish line, an arrival at peace and wholeness. I imagined it as a bed of roses—soft, fragrant, untainted. But days later, reality pressed in, and I realized healing was not the absence of struggle but the presence of God amid it.

I felt like a fragile bud, straining to push through the thorns of doubt, desperate for a single ray of light to reassure me that I could bloom. But those thorns, those sharp remnants of past trials, had wrapped around me for years. They spoke louder than truth, suffocating my courage, silencing my spirit. And I was afraid—terrified, even—because deep down, I wasn't sure I had the strength to fight my own self-doubt. It was easier to surrender to the familiar whispers of inadequacy than to believe that God saw something worthy in me. The past had become more than a memory—it was a fortress. My comfort, my defense. My walls.

Yet, even in that fear, even in the uncertainty, I now see the quiet work of healing. Because healing is not the absence of struggle—it is learning to trust God in the midst of it. It's choosing, day by day, to believe that His truth is stronger than the lies, that His love is deeper than my wounds and when I feel unworthy, He still calls me His.

And that, my friend, is the kind of healing that doesn't just mend—it transforms.

I realized that my reluctance to forge ahead signaled to God I wasn't ready to trust Him—or to let His healing reach deeper. Struggle had become a part of my daily life; it was all I knew. Letting go meant facing something difficult: the possibility that my life had value. I felt healing driving forward, at times almost out of control. I struggled to allow its full grasp. The voices of friends echoed in my ears, "Jesus loves you. Jesus cares for you.

Jesus died for you." I resisted their reach. I mocked their compassion—unintentionally pushing away every rescue attempt. Seriously, Jesus could use *me*? How could He use someone with a past like mine? Why would He want to?

What I hadn't yet realized was that God's healing had already started, and He was working to make me whole. Was I ready to walk in wholeness? We pray for it so easily... but once it comes, do we walk in its purpose? As surely as Jesus rose from the dead, my ashes began to rise from the grave. I saw a window of opportunity opening before me—to change, to chase after everything I'd once searched for, even dared to dream of. Would this Jesus really be everything I had heard, or would this be the end of my story? I knew I'd never have a better chance than at this moment—to jump in with both feet, to go all in. So, I did. I began devouring the truth of God's Word—it became oxygen to my soul. The truth cut deep, slicing through layers of doubt, gently soothing my aching, nearly lifeless spirit, crying for existence. The Word of God spoke to my hardened heart, and God's presence refreshed my soul. It happened so unexpectedly. Little by little, the pain began to ease... And God's plan began to unfold.

Imagine my shock when Pastor approached with news: I was going to be a Sunday School teacher. Me? A teacher? Wait—What? It hadn't even been a year since the conference. How could I possibly teach? Although I questioned my ability, the following week I found me standing beside Wayne, my husband, in the Sunday School room. We looked around in

dismay and asked, "Who would want to be in this classroom?"
Four white walls with little decoration, no excitement—Nothing.
I found myself drifting with adverse emotions and thought,
"What am I doing here?" Awakening me from my thoughts,
Wayne announced, "This won't do." I quickly agreed, assuming
he had sensed my reluctance. He continued, "We need to change
this up. We need to decorate." "Decorate?" What was he saying?
I responded, "Do what?" "This room needs inspiration." he
replied. And just like that, something shifted. Excitement rose as
we discussed the ideas that began to form from our enthusiasm.
We decided to build a jungle—a massive tree, a missionary hut
and animals everywhere. To my surprise, the more we worked,
the more my anticipation grew. We worked fervently with the
expectation that I would be the best teacher I could be. We
poured ourselves into it, determined to give our best. Maybe I
wouldn't be the greatest teacher... But I was willing to give what
little I had.

Then the day arrived—my first Sunday to teach. The room
was finished, far beyond our expectations, and I had studied,
prayed and prepared what I believed was an amazing lesson.
Children began pouring in but wait... Why was the room full?
There were more children than I had planned for. Quickly, I
asked, "Did everyone bring a visitor?" To which one young boy
replied, "No, I don't belong in this class, but I do now."
Unfortunately, I had to return the young child to his assigned
class, as tears streamed from his face. Although unfortunate for
him, I sensed a growing anticipation as something remarkable
was unfolding. Within weeks, other teachers began to embrace

the vision. It was as if a fresh wind of creativity blew through the Sunday School department, and within a few short months, every room was different. A vision had been cast. And although I was still fearful of teaching... I heard the Lord whisper, "You got this."

During my time co-teaching, I was introduced to a very kind-hearted individual named Donna—whom I soon would call "friend". She was placed in my life, to encourage, edify, and help build the kind of relationships I didn't realize I needed. Friendships within the church began to form—connections that brought laughter, love, and a sense of fellowship I hadn't experienced before. I'll admit now: it was a gift whose true value I wouldn't fully understand for years to come. Little by little, I found myself cracking open the door of my heart—if only slightly. Somehow, Donna reached deep, and before long, we became the best of friends... and prayer partners. Thankfully, she would be the first of many "teachers" God would send to reach inside my walls and speak life into my heart.

I will never forget the night I called Donna in anguish, struggling to understand the trial I was facing. I felt misplaced—unable to sense God's presence. It was as if His voice had gone silent. Desperately, I longed to feel Him—or at least hear his voice—even if just a whisper. I had been praying for weeks, pleading with God to answer. I cried out, "God, are You there?" Had I done something to anger Him? Had I done something wrong? Why was my heart so hard? I explained to Donna that I had reached my limit. Without hesitation, she said, "Let's meet

17

at the church." Frustrated, I thought to myself, "*What will it hurt?*" Arriving at the church a few hours later, Donna said, "Let's pray." "That's the problem. I have been praying. God doesn't hear me!" I grumbled. She didn't argue. She merely responded, "Then sit down, I will pray." I observed Donna as she knelt at the altar and earnestly sought answers through prayer. After about an hour of prayer, she stood and asked, "Do you feel Him?" "No." I whispered. Without a word, she turned back to the altar and continued in prayer. This cycle repeated itself for hours, each time she asked, I whispered: "No." Then something began to stir. The next time she asked, I said "Maybe." Within a few moments... I broke. Tears streamed down my face as I felt a touch. I looked up, startled—but no one was there except Donna. And she was still at the altar, lost in prayer. It couldn't have been her. But I *knew* I felt someone. We continued to pray through the night... losing all track of time.

When morning came, another teacher—hoping to get some work done in her classroom—entered the church. As she opened the door, she heard a cry and headed toward the sanctuary to investigate. Stepping through the main sanctuary doors, she saw Donna and me still praying. But something made her pause. Sensing someone else was there, she scanned the room. Then she heard something—footsteps overhead, coming from the balcony. She made her way upstairs, searching for the source of the sound she had just heard—but instead, she found herself overwhelmed. Tears streamed down her face as she fell to her knees before the Lord.

"Angels!" she declared a few days later. "It was ministering angels."

And I knew she was right. I had felt them too. I had felt the presence of the Lord that night—strong and undeniable. Barriers had fallen; walls which I had struggled to conquer for years had come crashing down.

It was a night I will never forget—*a night we entertained angels unaware.*

Over time, I came to realize that Donna had been strategically placed in my life to teach me the importance of prayer. She became a faithful prayer partner—someone who would walk beside me through some of the hardest seasons of my life. A true friend who prayed *with* me, and for me, and who gently encouraged my deeper walk with God. Her impact changed my life forever. I'll be the first to admit, her friendship confused me in the beginning. She wasn't family—at least not by blood. Why was she so kind? So compassionate? I couldn't comprehend her unconditional love... not then. It would take years before I truly appreciated the gift she was.

I had to learn something that few abuse survivors understand right away: Love can be terrifying. For many of us, the word "love" was twisted by pain. It was worldly love—a distorted, self-serving version of love—that wounded us in the first place. For me, it came from a stepdad who used words like, "It's because I love you," to ease his own conscience. The next thing I remember was the beating that followed. "You're too hard. You

19

need to be broken. You need to cry! If you cry, I'll stop the beating." I still remember that day—because something deep inside me took hold. *"I will not cry. You will not break me. I am not weak,"* I thought, bracing myself as blow after blow came. I thought I was winning. Refusing to back down, I believed I had proven something. I would *never* be weak again. But what I didn't realize was... there was no battle to win. All I had done was give permission for hardness to take root deep within my soul. A stubbornness that I thought would keep me from being a victim—but one that would later become a stumbling block that nearly destroyed me.

Thankfully, Donna's friendship began to break through some of that hardness. She explained that when we allow ourselves to be weak in God, that's when He draws the closest—an opportunity for divine embrace that I had unknowingly shut out for years. Little by little, Donna chipped away at my stubbornness, uncovering hidden walls I didn't even know were there—walls that came crashing down the night angels ministered to my weary, aching soul.

The next year, Wayne joined the teaching department as we took another step forward—this time to help with the Children's Church Division. Excitement began to grow, because we had always shared a love for children. We loved dressing up as different characters and adding extra flair to the weekly lessons. And that brought back memories of how it began. We were attending a church that needed volunteers for their upcoming Harvest Fest. Excitedly, someone suggested, "Wayne would make a great clown!" Anxiously, my husband and I looked at one another in quiet despair. We hadn't volunteered—not because we didn't want to, but because we were struggling financially. We were a young couple with three children. Our youngest son, Tyler, had been sick—almost living at Children's Hospital—which made it difficult to do anything extra. Sensing our hesitation, a friend offered to make a clown outfit for Wayne if we promised to help. Eager to be included, we quickly agreed. Soon however, our hopes were dashed when that same friend handed us the costume and said, "That will be one hundred dollars." One hundred dollars? We didn't have it—and clearly, that showed—because another friend immediately stepped in and replied, "I'll pay for it... if Wayne will perform at my daughter's birthday party. He'll make a great clown." With no other option, he agreed. Wayne panicked, as he had no idea how to be a clown. But surprisingly, it came naturally. And the birthday party? It was a complete success. What we thought was a small accomplishment soon became a step in growing a business. Wayne began to book parties, cultivating his talents—learning illusions, balloon art, and ventriloquism. Talents that would later serve the very children's ministry God was beginning to form.

A few years later, Wayne and I decided to visit our children at a summer church camp. We'd always loved the idea of working with children, and we wanted to see how the camp was run. Excitement heightened as we stepped onto the campgrounds—children were everywhere. What was this feeling? We instantly felt at home, like we belonged. We decided to stay for the night service, and anticipation grew as the time

approached. The service was just what we'd hoped for—
absolutely amazing. Children laughed, and God moved in ways
we had never seen before... through blacklight puppets. We had
never experienced a puppet show like this. Puppets shaped like
lightbulbs, glowed under the blacklight radiantly and danced
across the stage to the crowd's delight. To say we were
impressed would be an understatement. We were inspired.
Looking at each other, we proclaimed, "If we ever work with
children at this level, we *have* to do blacklight." That day,
something new was born in us—a desire for puppet ministry.
And with it, another piece of our life's puzzle slid into place.

Three: The Disconnect

Survival Mode: The Cost of Disconnection

*A*t times, Wayne and I hesitated to trust God—to surrender to His will for our lives. We brushed it off as inconvenient. We convinced ourselves we were too busy. But the truth? It unsettled us. It nudged us out of our comfort zone. In those moments, we found ourselves tempted to turn away—to ignore God. Hoping He would simply withdraw. And yet, He never did.

When He persisted, we rationalized our reluctance with insecurity, fear, and a deep sense of inadequacy. Maybe, just maybe, we believed that God was calling us to something beyond our abilities—something impossible. But Jesus said, *"Everything is possible for one who believes." Mark 9:23 NIV*

If *everything is* possible, then the disconnect isn't with God. It's with us—with our belief. That was the moment we recognized the true struggle. That's when we arrived at what we now call "The Disconnect."

It felt impossible when we sensed God calling us to move to another state. This change would push us far outside our comfort zone—stretching our faith as He continued to shape His ministry within our lives. Uncertain yet trusting in His guidance, we stepped forward, reluctantly but obediently. Doors opened swiftly, and direction unfolded before us. Yet, what we didn't realize at the time was that we had found a church—a place that would eventually birth an incredible Children's Ministry. First, though, God's healing had work to do.

Looking back, we saw the fear we carried. We longed to be accepted, loved and understood, yet struggled to believe that love was truly for us. Isolated in a new place with no family or friends close by, we felt like outsiders looking in. Our struggle wasn't because the church failed us—but because we resisted every offer of fellowship. Wounded by past experiences, we built walls around our hearts, shutting out the very community we yearned to be part of. All we really wanted was to belong, to find a family in faith. Yet, how could we embrace the warmth of belonging when we had been rejected by our own families? But how could we become part of a church family... when we kept pushing away every hand that reached out?

Burdened by a deep-seated lack of self-worth, we resigned ourselves to merely existing within the congregation, blending into the background rather than forging connections. Relationships felt like something we weren't meant to build, so we took solace in the busyness around us, content to remain unseen. Happiness felt unattainable—an elusive dream meant for others. Yet, something shifted when we were asked to serve in the children's department. The invitation sparked excitement, a rare flicker of confidence that urged us forward. We eagerly accepted, finding solace in a space where we felt both needed and capable. Finally, we had a place to thrive, a challenge to embrace.

When entrusted with leading the Sunday service, our enthusiasm swelled. Determined to make it an extraordinary experience, we poured ourselves into preparation. Secretly, behind the scenes, we set to work in our garage, constructing an intricate Western frontier, our own little town complete with a jailhouse, country store, and every detail meticulously crafted. We worked tirelessly. Each nail was hammered, each brushstroke applied with devotion. When the weekend finally arrived, we held our breath, eager yet hesitant. Keeping our surprise under wraps, we simply requested extra time for setup. On the Saturday before, we arrived early at the church, completing the stage and finalizing every last touch. As we stepped back, marveling at what we had created, a wave of satisfaction washed over us. It was better than we had imagined.

That night was restless, anticipation buzzing in our veins like the night before Christmas. The moment had finally arrived. We walked into the church the next morning, hearts pounding, only to be met with something incredible—pure, unfiltered gratitude. The director and pastor were beyond shocked—they were thrilled with the room and its transformation, their astonishment quickly turning into delight. "I never expected this," the director murmured, eyes shining. "This is wonderful."

Then came the children—wide-eyed, laughing, their excitement dispelling every doubt that had plagued us in the days prior. Their joy became our validation, their awe a reminder of why we had poured so much of ourselves into this. And then, the greatest compliment of all: after the service, they gathered around us, beaming. "That was fun! We loved it! We love you!"

Several little arms reached out, wrapping us in embraces of gratitude. I watched Wayne glow, his entire being radiating exhilaration and certainty. I knew, in that moment, that he had found his true calling—his purpose.

The hugs, however, were more complicated for me. Touch had been a source of pain in my past, something I had learned to fear rather than welcome. Yet, these embraces were different. They carried no weight of harm or obligation. They were simple, pure, and untainted by the wounds of the past. Perhaps, I thought, healing could be found in moments like this.

Soon, we were placed on a monthly rotation to continue our work in the Children's Department. Each session brought new opportunities to develop creative programs, and while crafting lessons that could truly captivate the children was sometimes a challenge, it was one we welcomed wholeheartedly. More than anything, our desire was to impart the Word of God—to plant seeds of faith and nurture a deep, lasting relationship between the children and their Creator.

One particular lesson still makes me laugh. We had devised an illustration using popcorn to demonstrate the power of the Holy Ghost. The idea was simple: as the kernels transformed and expanded under heat, it would symbolize how the Spirit moves in our lives, bringing change and growth—something the children could see, hear, and smell. It was meant to be a dynamic object lesson. What we hadn't considered was the sheer unpredictability of the process. As Wayne delivered what I must admit was a stirring message, I noticed the popcorn beginning to pop wildly out of control. Kernels flew in every direction, bouncing off tables, chairs, and even the children themselves. Alarmed, I rushed to cover the pot with a lid, only for Wayne— quick on his feet—to grab my hand and exclaim, "Don't quench the Spirit!" The room erupted into laughter. Though the lesson turned into an unexpected spectacle, it was in that moment that I realized something profound: Ministry isn't about flawless execution. Sometimes, the messiest experiences hold the greatest truths. God doesn't require perfection—He simply calls us to be willing, and He will turn even our disasters into meaningful teaching moments.

As our passion for ministry deepened, so did our creativity. Our western frontier set had served us well, but we sensed the need for something fresh—something that would inspire awe and keep the children eager to return. After much brainstorming, we decided on an ambitious new theme: a grand ship sailing with a lighthouse guiding the way. Excited, we rushed to our local home improvement store, eagerly gathering supplies and, right there in the middle of the aisle, we began assembling a miniature lighthouse. The confused glances from passing customers were amusing, but one man, unable to contain his curiosity, stopped and asked, "I've got to know—what are you building?" His intrigue quickly turned into enthusiasm as we explained our vision, and his parting words—"Those are some lucky children"—felt like yet another confirmation that we were on the right path. Back at the church, we were thrilled to find other team members already gathered, ready to help. They wanted to be part of what God was doing, and for days, we worked together, laughing, constructing, and creating an experience that would transport children to the Sea of Galilee, walking alongside Jesus and delving into the wonders of His Word.

Yet, amid the excitement, something unexpected happened. While assisting a young woman named Cassie in loading her mother into the car one evening, she leaned in close and whispered, *"When you tire of hiding behind the laughter, I am here."* The words hit me like a sudden gust of wind. Hiding behind the laughter? What did she mean? I forced a smile, gave a lighthearted goodbye, and hurried back to work, but the weight of her statement lingered. She had struck a truth I hadn't yet admitted to myself—I had been hiding behind the laughter, behind the busyness of ministry. Keeping my schedule packed gave me a sense of purpose, but beneath it all, there was an undeniable loneliness. I had spent years holding people at arm's length. It was easier that way. Friendship was fine, but boundaries? Absolutely necessary. I didn't realize how visible my guarded heart had become, but Cassie saw it, and now, her words haunted me. I avoided her—purposefully altering my path at church events, taking the longer route to avoid passing by her in hallways. But one day, during an altar call, she found me. Without hesitation, she knelt beside me at my pew, took my hand, and together, we prayed. As tears streamed down my face, something in me shifted—a pressure valve loosening just enough to let go of what I had been holding in for so long. "No expectations, no pressure, let's just be friends," she whispered.

Walking out of church that day, I felt something I hadn't in years—excitement. Not the kind that comes from a well-executed lesson or a new set design, but from the simple realization that I had found a friend. A real friend. No pretense, no masks, just companionship. From that day forward, our families grew close. We shared meals, played games, laughed wholeheartedly, and in those moments, I understood the true beauty of fellowship. For the first time in a long time, I knew—I was no longer alone. That family gave us the gift of Fellowship.

One evening, we decided to attend a health fair hosted by our church—a gathering designed to promote healthier living, complete with educational sessions and a light snack to conclude the night. As we sat alone at a table, we once again felt the sting of displacement. Around us, groups of friends laughed and enjoyed fellowship, a reminder that our close friends had recently moved away, leaving us feeling somewhat abandoned. That feeling was about to change, though not in the way we expected. While waiting for our table to be served, we noticed the side door of the fellowship hall crack open slightly. A man slipped inside and hurried toward our table, moving with quiet urgency, as if hoping to go unnoticed. He reached us and whispered, "Did anyone see me?" "I don't think so," I replied. "Good. I feel better," he said. Better? How could he feel better? The health fair had sparked all sorts of conversations about life choices and personal accountability, making me reflect deeply. "I don't feel better. If anything, I feel guilty. This fair really makes you think," I admitted. "Oh, it made me think too," the mystery man smirked. "Made me think I needed a better snack." With a sheepish grin, he confessed that he had quietly slipped away from the event to run across the street and grab a slice of lemon meringue pie. The table erupted into laughter as the funny little stranger introduced himself as Brother Richard. Though we had never met him before that night, life's struggles would soon intertwine our families—relationships that would have a profound impact on our lives.

We loved the church and soon found comfort in our Sunday School class, where we began forming friendships with other families. And yet, the Lord must have sensed lingering hesitation in our hearts. We were beginning to trust—but only from a safe distance. We had much to offer but remained hesitant, until one

Sunday morning when an unexpected moment pushed us toward deeper faith and connection. Running late for Sunday School, we sped toward church when I noticed an elderly woman pacing around her car, a look of confusion on her face. Instinctively, I hit the brakes and began to turn around. "What are you doing?" Wayne asked. "I think she needs help," I said. "She's probably just stretching her legs," Wayne countered. "Maybe so, but it's spitting snow. We need to make sure she's okay." My concern was confirmed when she explained that she had run out of gas. Though she insisted she would be fine, we persuaded her to get into our vehicle. Since we weren't far from home, we had a gas can handy, allowing us to quickly get her back on the road. Given the freezing temperatures, it was too risky for her to wait alone, so she reluctantly agreed. Within an hour, she was safely on her way again.

Of course, our good deed had now made us even later for class. I explained to Wayne that we would need to sneak in quietly to avoid disrupting the lesson. But I should have known better. After all, I had married a goofball. As we arrived at church, Wayne threw open the classroom door and declared, "All rise!" My face turned every shade of red imaginable, while the class burst into laughter.

To my relief, Sis. Regina, the Sunday School teacher's wife, waved us in and called out, "Get in here, you two!" Though I was thoroughly embarrassed, something shifted that day. Before, we had found fellowship on a small scale—but that moment opened the door to something greater. Through that class, we

31

formed close bonds with different families and the incredible teaching team, the Singers. Through their guidance, we grew spiritually, strengthening our faith not only through the study of God's Word but also through gatherings, class parties, and shared experiences.

Once again, we were on cloud nine—until one morning, everything changed. The announcement shattered our hearts: The Singers were stepping down, and a new couple—the Spears family—would take their place. The class had become more than a routine; it was a refuge, a place where we found strength and solace each week. And now, it was slipping away. Anger welled up inside me, and I turned my frustration toward God. "Why? Every time we find comfort. You change it up." I felt abandoned, almost betrayed. We had been growing spiritually, finding our footing within the church, only to have it pulled out from under us. I pleaded with Sister Regina not to leave, hoping she would reconsider. But she only reassured me, "Everything will be okay." I wasn't convinced. Frustration burned in my chest, and I knew—deep down—I would resist opening up again.

Why allow myself to get close to someone, only for them to walk out of my life once more? To say I struggled with the change would be an understatement—I wrestled with it. Then the inevitable day arrived. The new teachers stepped in, and I— gripped by bitterness—held back, silent. Frustration smothered my laughter. Even my prayers felt hollow. Sister Spear must have sensed something was off. She was gentle, kindhearted, yet different from the people I usually allowed into my life. Soft-spoken but commanding respect, she piqued my curiosity. Something about her was unlike anyone I had ever known. But what was it? It would take months before I understood why God had placed them in our lives.

Then came the day that changed everything. It began like any other. My suitcase was packed, ready for yet another flight to Austin, Texas. My company had acquired a new business, and my role was to train the staff. This wasn't my first trip—I had been traveling for months, wrapping up the final details of the account. Wayne had already dropped me off at the airport. As I checked my bags, my phone rang—a number I didn't recognize. Assuming it was work-related, I answered. "This is Sergeant Thomas," a sharp voice barked. "You need to get home immediately." Confused, I hesitated. "Home? Why? What's going on?" "It's your oldest daughter. There's been a situation. We need you to meet us at the hospital—now." The world around me seemed to blur. "What happened?" I pressed, but he offered no details. I didn't wait to find out. Wayne and I rushed home and drove straight to the hospital. As we entered, the sheer number of police officers crowding the room stunned us.

Confusion gripped me as I scanned the scene, seeking answers. Then I saw her. "Momma, I didn't think you would come." Her words stopped me cold. "Where else would I be?" I asked, reaching for her. Before I could touch her, Sergeant Thomas intervened, escorting us out of the room. And then—he spoke the words that would freeze time itself. "Your daughter attempted suicide." Everything around me ceased to exist. "Did you hear me?" His voice was sharp, pulling me back. "Yes, I heard you," I whispered. "I just don't believe you." Shock blurred my reality. My thoughts spun wildly between denial and disbelief as we were interrogated, pressed for answers we didn't have. And though he eventually seemed satisfied with our responses, we were left drowning in confusion.

Suicide? What had she been thinking? Life wasn't perfect, but it was far from unbearable. Concern twisted into anger. How dare anyone question us as parents? We love our children—they were our world. Had she truly not understood her worth in our lives?

The physician on duty informed us that we would not be allowed in the room while they conducted their investigation. His words were firm yet laced with the weight of urgency. He instructed us to sit in the waiting room, explaining that it would take several hours—we needed to settle in and make ourselves comfortable. But there was no comfort to be found in that sterile hospital waiting area. No refuge in its stiff chairs and white-washed walls. The air felt thick, suffocating. Overwhelmed beyond words, I knew I couldn't stay. The weight of waiting was unbearable. Without hesitation, I rose and walked out of the hospital. Wayne's voice trailed after me, laced with confusion. He called out, "Where are you going?" "It's Wednesday night." I barked in response. "Church has started," my voice sharp and cutting. For me, facing the situation alone was impossible. My mind swirled with endless questions, each demanding answers that were nowhere to be found. But in my heart, I knew—God was up to something, and I needed to find out what.

Sliding into the back row of the church, I felt the weight of every pair of eyes upon me. The service had already begun, yet my presence had disrupted the rhythm of worship. Friends exchanged knowing glances, their expressions mirroring the unspoken question—I was supposed to be on a flight to Austin, not here. But I couldn't be anywhere else. Not now. The pain in my head was unbearable, throbbing with each beat of my heart. I could barely sit still. The walls of the sanctuary felt too close, pressing in around me. I had to escape. I slipped out of the auditorium and into a quiet Sunday School room, desperate to be alone with God. Wayne followed; his worry etched deep into his face. Sister Jen, the Children's Church director, was close behind him, both trying to reassure me—offering words of comfort, reminders that God was in control. Their voices blurred, drowned beneath the tidal wave of my own turmoil. Before I could respond, nausea overtook me. My body convulsed with sickness, the stress manifesting in uncontrollable waves. Sister Jen rushed to grab a waste can, gently comforting me, wiping my brow with a damp cloth as my body betrayed me. "Just breathe" she urged, her voice soothing, steady. "It's going to be okay." And then—music. Soft at first, then swelling, filling every corner of the room. The presence of God surrounded me, wrapping itself around my weary soul. I stumbled to my feet as Wayne and Sister Jen tried to keep me seated, but I couldn't stay still. I couldn't ignore it. I had to respond. I had to be in His presence.

Returning to the auditorium, I saw the altar call had already begun. Several individuals knelt in prayer; their faces turned toward Heaven. My heart pulled me forward. My body resisted, weak from exhaustion, but I pressed on. Each step felt heavier than the last, but I knew—I had to reach Him. I wanted to fall to my knees, to cry out, to pour every ounce of my sorrow onto that sacred ground. Before I could, Sister Bishop, my pastor's wife, grabbed hold of my legs and cried out to God on my behalf. The church sensed something was wrong. They didn't ask questions, didn't demand explanations. They simply gathered around, lifting their voices in unified prayer.

Pastor Bishop spoke, his voice steady, unwavering. "This family needs prayer. We don't need details; we just need to pray." We had called him enroute to the hospital, asking him and his wife to take our youngest daughter, shielding her from whatever horror awaited us. We couldn't let her be part of this unknown battle. As the prayers of the saints rose, something shifted. Strength seeped into my weary bones, though my sobs remained uncontrollable. I didn't care what anyone thought. My girl was hurting, and I was helpless to ease her pain.

She didn't understand—she was everything to me. The very reason I had found God. She was a miracle, though in her own eyes, she believed she was nothing but a mistake. No words could convince her otherwise. She had and always would hold a place in my heart—a sacred space she wouldn't fully comprehend until weeks later.

Realizing I had to return to the hospital, I offered heartfelt thanks to everyone who had prayed and turned to leave. But God had bigger plans—ones I would not understand in that moment. Just as I was about to step away, Sis. Spear gently grabbed my arm, her gaze steady and unwavering. "You don't have to go back alone," she said. "We're going with you." Her words caught me off guard. Though I knew the gravity of the situation, I hesitated. "It's okay, truly. You don't need to go," I assured her. "We want to go," she insisted. I glanced at Bro. Spear, whose nod confirmed their resolve. I knew there was no persuading her otherwise—her determination was unshakable. Though I felt like an inconvenience, I couldn't deny the quiet relief washing over me. We wouldn't have to face this trial alone.

When we arrived back at the hospital, the news shattered what little steadiness I had left—our daughter was being transported to another facility. She would undergo treatment there, and we had no say in the matter. Instinctively, I reached for her, desperate to offer comfort. She was visibly distraught; her face flushed with fear. But before I could wrap my arms around her, the sheriff stepped forward, blocked my way and forced me from the room. Even now, her words haunt me. "I'm sorry, Momma. I'm sorry." The weight of her voice, tremulous and aching, sent a pain through me unlike anything I had ever known. I could feel the terror in her trembling frame, mirroring the uncertainty that gripped my own heart. What would become of her? Why were we being torn from her life? What had we done to deserve this nightmare?

The officers informed us that following the ambulance was not an option—we would have to find our own way to the new hospital. Seeing our devastation, the Spears family did not hesitate. "You are in no shape to drive," Sis. Spear said firmly. "We'll take you." The journey stretched long into the night, the minutes dragging as we navigated an unfamiliar road toward an uncertain future. When we finally arrived, it was well past midnight. Finding an admitting hospital had taken longer than expected. We were ushered through the psychiatric ward, an unsettling contrast to the overwhelming storm in my mind. The atmosphere was thick with a quiet, eerie tension. The dim glow of fluorescent lights cast strange shadows on the walls, making the space feel even more foreign. It was almost as if my surroundings mirrored my emotions—confusion, dread, and a deep, relentless ache.

Lost in thought, I suddenly noticed something shift in the corner of my vision. My breath caught. "That bed over there—it just moved," I whispered, unnerved. We had thought we were alone. Brother Richard Spear, sensing the weight of the moment, seized the opportunity to break the silence. With a quick-witted remark, he cracked a joke—something lighthearted and unexpected. To my surprise, I felt the corners of my lips lift. A smile. Small, fleeting, but real. What I didn't realize then was that God was preparing us for one of the most grueling nights of our lives.

The next few hours were merciless. Question after question, meeting after meeting—we were raked over the coals, forced to relive every painful detail. Each interrogation stripped us raw, leaving us hollow and disoriented. Then, just as swiftly as the night had unraveled, the meeting was over. "It's time to leave," they informed us. "No!" My voice rang out, fierce with conviction. "I will not leave! If my girl stays, I stay." My hands trembled, but my stance did not waver. I would not abandon her.

The brutal reality of our situation crashed down as the nurse and security guard pried our daughter from our arms. She burst into tears, her sobs echoing down the sterile corridor as they ushered her away. Our own cries mingled with hers, helpless and broken, as the heavy metal doors slammed shut between us. "I'm sorry, I'm so sorry," she wailed. Those words—sharp, aching—lodged themselves in my heart like a blade. Perhaps they could separate us physically, but mentally, we remained rooted to that hospital floor, unwilling to leave. The doctor tried to reassure us, telling us she would be okay, that we should go home and rest. But how could we? Sensing our anguish, the Spears family gently urged us to let them take us home. "You need to rest," they pleaded. I shook my head. "We can't," I whispered. "That's our girl. She needs us." Every ounce of strength had drained from our bodies, yet the thought of leaving felt impossible. Sis. Spears took my hand, her voice soft but resolute. "Please. Let us take you home."

Tears blurred my vision as I murmured, "We can't. We don't even have the strength to move." Smiling through her own tears, she squeezed my hand. "That's where we come in." With quiet determination, she and Richard took hold of Wayne and I, guiding us step by step out of the hospital. That moment—a silent act of love and friendship—was exactly what God had intended for our bond. It was a friendship forged through ministry, one whose true significance we wouldn't fully grasp until years down the road.

Back home, rest remained elusive. The house felt hollow, too quiet, too heavy with absence. Drawn to our daughter's room, we stepped inside only to find a folded note lying next to her class ring. With trembling hands, I unfolded the letter. She had written an apology, pouring out the depths of her struggle— one that, in many ways, mirrored our own. Could we still love the fractured shell of the girl she had become? Lost in her search for love, she had chased a world that only wounded her, a world we had failed to understand until it was too late. She wore masks, shaping herself into what she thought love should be, but none of it was ever enough. With each disappointment, her anger grew. She had expected the world to fill the void in her heart, not realizing that only God could.

The weight of it crushed me. I couldn't sit still another moment. Tossing the note aside, I stood abruptly. "I'm going back to the hospital." Wayne, weary but worried, pleaded with me. "Please. You need to rest." Rest? How could I sleep knowing our daughter was drowning in pain? Grabbing a bag, I hastily stuffed it with clothes and a few personal items for her. My hands shook as I turned the ignition, my mind clouded by grief. As I drove, something inside me broke—a dam holding back years of unspoken emotion burst wide open. Sobs racked my chest as I cried out to God, pleading, demanding, searching. Anger. Heartache. Helplessness. How could she not see how much we loved her? Did she even realize how desperately we needed her? Blame crept in, twisting like a vice around my thoughts. Had I failed her? Was my own struggle with love part of her battle? Where had everything gone so terribly wrong?

Back at the hospital, I forced myself to take a few deep breaths, calming my emotions. I had to be strong—for her. She needed to know we would fight for her, that she wasn't alone in this. But when I arrived, I was met with cold resistance. "You can't see her," the doctor said. "Not yet." The words hit like a punch to the gut. I handed over her belongings, praying they would bring her comfort. "When can we visit?" I asked, my voice barely more than a whisper. "We'll be in touch in a few days." Days?

The next few days dragged endlessly, each moment agonizing. Sleep was a stranger, and food felt meaningless. We sat in silence, minds spinning, searching for answers that refused to come. We confronted the school, desperate for insight, only to learn that Brittany had confided in a counselor—someone who had known she was struggling and yet had never reached out to us. Anger boiled in my chest.

We called friends, family—anyone who might have seen or known something we had missed. How had we overlooked her cries? Understanding the importance of our children's emotional well-being, we knew it was critical to check in with her siblings to ensure they were coping. They were not. Each struggled with a torrent of emotions as they tried to comprehend their sister's choices. They wrestled with confusion, anger, and heartbreak. Over the next few days, we had tough conversations—about fear, pain, and the uncertainty that loomed over us all. It was a sobering reality check, forcing us to confront difficult questions and emotions that had long remained unspoken.

In looking inward, we admitted there were struggles in our own lives—challenges that, if left unresolved, could hinder our ability to truly support our children. How could they understand if we ourselves struggled? But giving up was never an option. Wasn't that the essence of faith—to trust that God would guide us through even the darkest moments?

As difficult as it was to be vulnerable with our children, something profound happened that week. Our relationships shifted. We acknowledged our imperfections as parents and embraced the necessity of open communication—not just for them, but for us all. In drawing closer, we experienced a transformation—one born from pain yet leading to a lasting change for good.

Anger surged through my heart, tangled with exhaustion and sorrow. I struggled to process the storm of emotions crashing over me. I was mentally, physically, and spiritually drained. The thought of eating, resting, or even moving felt impossible. How could I take comfort in simple things while our daughter was in that awful place? Wayne pleaded with me to take a bite of soup.

"Just one bite," he urged. I refused. Friends reached out, but I barely had the energy to pick up the phone. A week passed, and concern grew among those closest to us. Sensing the urgency, the Spears family decided to visit. The moment they walked into our home, their concern turned to certainty—Wayne and I did not look well. The weight of the situation had left its mark. "You have to eat," Sister Spears insisted gently. "The question now is—where?" Brother Spears chimed in, unwavering. "Anywhere you want. It's on us." "No," I whispered. I knew I needed food, but I had no strength, no desire. "We're not giving you a choice," Sister Spears asserted. "It's time to get dressed." Their kindness was relentless, and I knew they would not leave without seeing me take care of myself. Reluctantly, I agreed. A little soup might help, if only to quiet their concern. Every spoonful took effort, and swallowing felt nearly impossible. Yet Sister Spears continued to encourage me—reminding me that I needed my strength.

Days later, that truth became undeniable. We were summoned to see our daughter. Relief washed over us when we arrived at the hospital and saw our daughter rushing into our arms. She looked rested, even peaceful. Soon, a doctor entered the room and introduced himself. "So, you're the parents," he said with a knowing smile. "I've been following this closely. I called the school and spoke with the nurses. I've never seen two parents love their child as deeply as you love your daughter." His words caught us off guard. In the chaos of the past week, we hadn't paused to reflect on the depth of our actions. But there was little time to linger in the moment. The doctor turned to

Brittany and prompted her gently. "Go ahead. Talk to them."
Our daughter's eyes filled with tears as she looked at us, her
voice wavering. "I'm so sorry... for everything I put you
through," she whispered. Her words came hesitantly, carrying
the weight of emotions too heavy to bear alone. We reached for
her hand, holding on as we listened. "It's okay, baby," I
reassured her. Dr. Green encouraged her to continue. "I didn't
really attempt suicide," Brittany admitted. "I just wanted your
attention." The air shifted. Those words held gravity we hadn't
anticipated. She had our full attention now, and as she recounted
the events of that day, my heart ached to hear her struggle. Yet,
amidst the sorrow, I found immense pride in her courage—in her
willingness to be vulnerable, to trust us with her pain. The road
ahead would not be easy. But in that hospital room, healing had
begun—not just for our daughter, but for our family.

That chapter of our lives is difficult to speak about. Nearly
impossible—but God. To fully connect our lives to Him, we
must start at the very root of His nature. God is love.

*"And so we know and rely on the love God has for us. God
is love. Whoever lives in love lives in God, and God in them."*
1 John 1:46 NIV

Love is God's very essence—His DNA. It is the force that
suffered for us, bore our burdens, and gave itself entirely so that
we might experience it in full power. Love is patient and kind. It
does not envy, does not boast, and is not proud.

Love does not dishonor others, is not self-seeking, is not easily angered, and keeps no record of wrongs. Love does not delight in evil but rejoices in truth. Love protects, trusts, hopes, and perseveres. Love—God's love—never fails.

It is the same love we hold for our children. And no matter what trials life brings, we will face them together.

The Word of God declares,

"God is Love" 1 John 4:8.

But how do we truly grasp this divine truth? It begins within—an honest reckoning with ourselves and with God, a lesson I learned profoundly through our experience with our daughter, Brittany. To embrace God's love, we must lay aside all doubt, deception, and the urge to conceal the wounds of our past. Often, we find ourselves willing to admit—almost all—perhaps ninety percent of our struggles. But what of the remaining ten percent? Do we quiet our guilt by offering part of our hearts, convincing ourselves that some is better than none? Wrong.

The adversary of our souls delights in this deception. By withholding, we essentially say, "Lord, I trust You with only these pieces." Like a child offering a portion of his candy while secretly keeping the rest—we fool ourselves into thinking it is enough. But we know in our hearts God asks for all. He will not settle for fragments of our devotion. Scripture makes this clear:

"So, because you are lukewarm—neither hot nor cold—I am about to spit you out of my mouth." Revelation 3:16 NIV

True surrender demands completeness—one hundred percent. Anything less leaves room for the enemy's whispers: "What if someone knew? What if they saw? What if they heard?" It is tempting to pray that someone else might read our thoughts, speak our pain for us. But healing will not come until we walk through our fears ourselves. God calls us to a journey of wholeness, where our struggles are not meant to destroy but to refine us, shaping Christ-like character within.

Yet therein lies the challenge: Trust. How can we trust again after pain, rejection, and betrayal? We vowed never to reach out, never to risk vulnerability again. We trusted—and were hurt. We reached out—and were abandoned. We loved—and were rejected. But then comes the voice of the Lord, gentle yet firm: "Yes, but this time, let your trust be in Me."

"It is better to take refuge in the LORD than to trust in humans." Psalms 118:8 NIV

Man is flawed, capable of hurt—sometimes unintentionally. But our confidence is never meant to rest in people's responses; it must be anchored in the unwavering faithfulness of God. We can't retreat into isolation, for God doesn't call us to a life of seclusion. Our wounds may convince us to withdraw, to separate ourselves from the very encouragement He has provided. Yet, in doing so, we fall prey to the enemy's greatest lie—that distance will protect us, when in reality it is only a connection with God—that restores us.

Brittany, tragically, did not grasp her divine worth. She became disconnected—lost within herself—unable to see the love that surrounded her. She listened to the enemy's lies until her heart shut down. And isn't that the struggle we all face? If we give the enemy a voice in our lives, he will always push us toward disconnection from God.

So how do we begin to reconnect what has long been shut down? How do we allow ourselves to feel again—to accept touch, emotion, vulnerability—without fear? It starts by admitting one simple truth: *We want to feel again.* Yes, feelings bring both good and bad. And when the floodgates open, everything tends to come pouring out. But here's what we must remember—the good will outweigh the bad. God doesn't waste anything. God is at work in us, for His purpose:

> *"For it is God who works in you to will and to act in order to fulfill his good purpose."*—*Philippians 2:13 NIV*

Rather than resisting the pain, we embrace it. For in those raw, vulnerable moments, healing unfolds. And only then can God bring His will to fruition in our lives.

Before we step forward into battle, we must first prepare our heart. The enemy does not idly watch as we walk away from our pain, for he understands the vessel we can become in God's hands. More importantly, he knows that our trials today will one day transform into our testimony.

"They triumphed over him by the blood of the Lamb and by the word of their testimony; they did not love their lives so much as to shrink from death." Revelation 12:11 NIV

God's love is Holy, pure, and unshakably true. It is a love that no earthly force can imitate, improve upon, or parallel.

And so we know and rely on the love God has for us. God is love. Whoever lives in love lives in God, and God in them.— 1John 4:16 NIV

If God is love, then can He truly dwell within us if we refuse to love or be loved? Scripture speaks plainly—each of us must judge this truth for ourselves.

Too often, we reject the people God places in our lives, arguing against their presence rather than seeing His divine hand in our relationships. But can we truly reject God? We allow hurt feelings, pain, and bitterness to separate us from those around us, numbing our hearts, shutting down our emotions because it feels safer than confronting the truth of His Word.

"My command is this: Love each other as I have loved you. Greater love has no one than this: to lay down one's life for one's friends."—John 15:12-13 NIV

Love one another? Lord, if You knew the people around me, You would change Your mind. Didn't a traitor and a liar walk alongside Jesus? Wasn't one of His Apostles a deceiver—another a doubter? Who remained with Him in His darkest hour? Didn't those who called Him "friend" scatter when the path became too difficult? Yet Jesus still loved them? And it's the same with you and I. Consider Him—Has He ever abandoned us when we forsook, mocked, or turned away in rebellion? No, His love remains—unchanging, unbreakable, and unconditional.

> *"Be completely humble and gentle; be patient, bearing with one another in love." Ephesians 4:2 NIV*

We are commanded to love as He loved—not merely when we *feel* led to love. If love were dependent on our emotions, would we ever truly love as God intended? Perhaps that is why Jesus emphasized love so frequently, knowing our tendency to condition it upon convenience and comfort.

> *"Be devoted to one another in love. Honor one another above yourselves." Romans 12:10 NIV*

> *"Carry each other's burdens, and in this way you will fulfill the law of Christ." Galatians 6:2 NIV*

Our duty is to love—when it is difficult, when it is painful, when it defies logic. To truly know God is to love as He loves, for without His love, we risk the greatest *Disconnect* of all: believing that we can survive apart from Him or His love.

Four: The Elephant and the Frogs

When Pharaoh Lives in Me

*T*oo often, we settle for far less than what God offers. We accept our fate—or worse, we interpret our struggle as punishment, convinced we're too undeserving to hope for more. We hesitate to name the elephant in the room: shame. Shame weighs heavily, convincing us we are unworthy—unworthy to be loved, unworthy to be used, unworthy to be healed. We feel depleted, deflated, rejected, and undone, shackled by the labels the world places upon us. But what does God see? Who does God see? It is not about the world's perception—it's about God's. And on the Day of Judgment, will the world stand beside us? Will their perception justify our choices? I can almost see Jesus looking us in the eye, asking, "Was the world worth more than what I offered?" Scripture makes it clear:

"...don't you know that friendship with the world means enmity against God? Therefore, anyone who chooses to be a friend of the world becomes an enemy of God." James 4:4 NIV

At times, we allow the world to define our identity—defining who we are and who we become. We make excuses, accept their judgment and ignore the truth. We let the world offer convenient ways to sweep our struggles under the rug—as if what's hidden will simply go away. Our pain doesn't disappear just because we pretend it's not there. Every day, we carry our burdens... even if they're buried.

The world's solution? Avoidance. Hide it. Ignore it. Hope it fades. But the truth always lingers—and while the world may choose silence, God does not. Inward struggles are like a meerkat burrowing deep underground, creating a maze of tunnels with twists and turns—a desperate attempt at security. Yet, the same pathways that offer escape also leave openings for predators to strike. Ignorance and denial are mere illusions of safety. Real healing begins with truth.

"Therefore confess your sins to each other and pray for each other so that you may be healed. The prayer of a righteous person is powerful and effective." James 5:16 NIV

First, we must confess—acknowledge our difficulties and call them by name. We must confront the elephant in the room instead of pretending it doesn't exist. And once we recognize it, we must address the internal struggle by aligning ourselves with God's Word. God is willing—are we? I never realized my own

unwillingness until God opened a door I never expected. One
Sunday morning in class, Sister Spears introduced me to her dear
friend. With a bright smile, Sister Rachael extended her hand.
"My name is Rachael Asgari-Rad. You can remember that—like
a scary rod," she joked, bursting into laughter. Instantly, I felt a
kindred spirit—something in me just knew: *We were going to be
best friends.* And I was right. She became a friend I could
depend on—through the toughest and best of times. A living
example of what a best friend should be.

Within no time, the three of us—Sister Spears, Rachael, and
I—became inseparable. We sat together in Sunday School,
shared laughter, and embraced the joy of life. But what I didn't
know at the time was that they sensed something I wasn't ready
to admit—I was still holding back. Though they had drawn
close, something in me had quietly pressed the brakes. And the
depth of our friendship stalled... not from their side, but from
mine.

One evening, under the guise of a simple dinner, our night
took a turn I never saw coming. After dinner, Sister Spears
casually mentioned she needed to swing by the church to grab
something from her classroom. As we arrived, Sister Rachael
smiled and suggested, "Let's go with her—it'll give us time to
chat." My heart panicked. Chat? About what? I thought I had
concealed my struggles. What did they know?

Within minutes, I found myself sitting uncomfortably in a
corner, with the two positioned between me and the door. The

53

conversation began gently—slow, patient, deliberate. They weren't trying to push; they only wanted to know *me*. To my surprise, I relaxed. However, a quiet intimidation still lingered, their presence was gentle, and their intentions pure. For hours, we laughed, shared, and cried together. And with every exchange, the pressures within slowly released. Yet, I knew deep down I was still holding back—fearful of trust, hesitant because of past wounds. And so, I let myself believe a lie: That I only needed to release *just enough* to get by. What are we really signaling to God when we ignore the storm raging inside—when we refuse to trust Him with the burdens pressing down on our soul?

I hadn't realized how stubborn I had become—how much I was resisting God's help—until that night when He gently tugged at my heartstrings. Sleep eluded me as my mind churned with unspoken struggles. Why hadn't I been open about what I was feeling? Why did I hold back? Inwardly, I had longed for this very opportunity. But when it arrived…I let it slip through my fingers.

Discouraged, I found myself weeping. "Why, Lord?" I crawled out of bed, careful not to wake Wayne, but I couldn't stay there—I needed to clear my head. Settling into my recliner in the living room, I noticed my Bible sitting on the side table beside me. From past experiences, I knew reading God's Word had always brought peace. I opened it, and my eyes fell on the book of Exodus—Pharaoh's story. Why that passage? Why not

the comfort of Psalms? Wouldn't David understand my
lamenting better?

It's easy to read about biblical figures and judge their
choices. Pharaoh—stubborn, prideful, defiant. Most Christians
know the story by heart: "Let my people go." And Pharaoh
says... no. But have we ever stopped to consider *why*? What was
going on inside him? Pharaoh's resistance wasn't just rebellion,
it was pain and fear. It was a heart that had hardened over time,
layer by layer. Sound familiar? It did to me.

In Exodus Moses said to Pharaoh:

*(9) "I leave to you the honor of setting the time for me to
pray for you and your officials and your people that you and
your houses may be rid of the frogs, except for those that remain
in the Nile."*

*(10) "Tomorrow, Pharaoh said. Moses replied, It will be as
you say, so that you may know there is no one like the Lord our
God." Exodus 8:9-10, (NIV)*

Pharaoh responded, "Tomorrow."

Let's talk about these frogs. They were *everywhere*—in the
fields, in their homes, hopping down the streets, croaking in
beds, squatting in ovens, slithering across kitchen counters,
nesting in barns. This wasn't about a few harmless amphibians—
these were nerve-wracking, slimy, relentless creatures invading
every inch of Egypt. The sound must have been deafening. And

when they died? They were piled up high in rancid heaps, a rotting reminder of Pharaoh's refusal to surrender. Picture an Egyptian woman kneading dough—only to shriek as a frog leapt from her mixing

bowl. Imagine a child reaching for his coat—and pulling frogs from every pocket. The little boys probably loved it. The little girls? I can still hear their screams.

Now, imagine Pharaoh—his palace overrun; his every step met with a sickening *squish... squish... squish.* Eventually, even he couldn't take it anymore. He summoned Moses:

"Entreat the Lord, that He may take away the frogs from me, and from my people, and I will let the people go, that they may do sacrifice unto the Lord."

Finally. Pharaoh was ready to surrender. So, Moses asked: *"When shall I entreat for thee?"* And Pharaoh's answer? "Tomorrow." Seriously? Tomorrow? At this point, my patience with Pharaoh was thin. Was he out of his mind? His home—his entire kingdom—was crawling with frogs. And here was God, offering immediate relief. And yet, Pharaoh hesitated. And right then, God whispered softly to my heart: "How about your circumstance?" Before we condemn Pharaoh's foolish delay, let's be honest. How often have we told God, "Tomorrow."

We all have frogs in our lives—those burdens we carry day after day. The frogs of heartache, disappointment, uncertainty, sickness, and doubt. The frogs of suffering, sadness, depression, guilt. The relentless frogs of anger, grief, bitterness...resentment. And yet—despite the turmoil, despite God's open invitation to intervene—we still tell Him, "Tomorrow." We convince ourselves that waiting will help. That maybe time, on its own, will heal what only surrender can fix. But the truth? Our circumstances only worsen, our heartbreak deepens, our health declines, our faith weakens, our attitude sours. What are we thinking?

Why are we so afraid to trust Him—*today?* Why do we insist on one more day with the frogs? God is already standing by. And He asks the same question He once asked Pharaoh: "When do you want Me to take care of your frogs?"

I was just as defiant as Pharaoh—clinging to my fear and hesitation, even as God placed two friends in my life. Two caring individuals who cared enough to pause their schedules and minister to my aching heart. As I reflect on that conversation now, I realize it was the very opportunity I had prayed for... even dreamed of. And yet, when the moment came, I struggled to be transparent. I thought I was ready to reach for help, but the words caught in my throat. Speaking through the pain felt impossible.

I couldn't be authentic—not with myself, not with God. It was easier to keep the struggle buried than to risk exposing my heart and stepping forward. My deepest cries were silenced by doubt—crushed beneath the weight of fear and self-judgment. In truth... no one was judging me but me. As the conversation neared its end, relief flooded my heart—but underneath it, guilt whispered its name. Why did they care so much? Why would they take time from their lives to reach into mine? Anxiety told me: it would be easier to believe they could read my mind, understand without words. But that's not how God works. That's not His design. He didn't want me to remain hidden—He longed for me to trust the work He had already begun. And so, I wept. Not only had I failed to trust these friends completely, but I had denied God Himself. Through my tears, I repented and thanked Him for the opportunity, even though I had not embraced it as He intended. Yet, in my faltering, He was working. Healing, as I was learning, is not always instant—it is a journey. And that night—was another step forward.

In time, I began to recognize how God had quietly placed certain individuals in my life—people whose footprints I hadn't seen at first. But they were there. Guiding. Steady. Faithful. These two friends, once strangers, have since become my closest supporters. Though miles may separate us now, the moment we reunite, it's as if no time has passed at all. They have never judged me. Never condemned me. They have only loved me— for who I am, and for the masterpiece God is still creating within me. For them, I am endlessly grateful... and deeply blessed.

During my darkest moments, the enemy deceived me into believing I was alone. Completely alone—walking through life unseen and unsupported. But looking back, I saw the lie for what it was. Loneliness wasn't my reality. It was my fear. My reluctance. I was the one who pushed love away. I was the one who resisted the help God so graciously sent. And yet... in His infinite goodness, God never abandoned me. He kept sending lifeboats—faithful souls who reached out again and again. Some I rejected. Some I wounded, unknowingly, out of fear or confusion. For that, I offer my sincerest apology. Because the truth is—my heart longed for love. But not the kind I had known. Love—real, godly love—was still foreign to me. The only love I had ever been shown was warped, twisted into something that wounded instead of healed. I didn't know how to recognize the difference. How could I trust something called love when "love" had once justified my pain?

I recall a pastor's wife once asking me, "Why do some abused people reject love?" My answer came simply, but certain: "Because they were hurt in the name of love." It's hard to trust love when the world has perverted its meaning. When an abuser whispers, "I do this because I love you," in the middle of violence. When manipulation hides behind the hollow phrase, "I love you." That is not love, it is a distortion. A mockery of what love was ever meant to be. It took me years to learn the difference—to recognize that only God's definition of love is truth. His love does not wound—It heals.

I've made choices that resulted in lost friendships, decisions that created painful distances. Never intentionally—always as failed attempts to reach for something just beyond my grasp. I wish I could go back...rewrite the past...make better choices. But I can't. I must live with the consequences. And yet—even in those mistakes—God placed people in my path who were willing to go deeper, to push harder, to refuse to leave. I wanted to be truthful. To admit I didn't understand love. But fear of rejection and pain silenced me. So instead... I tested them. Believing, deep down, that if they truly loved me, they would fight for me. Because that's all the little girl inside me ever wanted— Someone who would fight for her. Someone who wouldn't walk away. As a child, no one saw me. No one noticed my silent battles. And now, as an adult, the pain had become part of me— woven into the fabric of my thoughts and actions. Although it was a distorted perception, it was the only perspective I had known at that time, and an issue that was deeply ingrained.

Why did I hold my heart so tightly? Even after I came to know God, I failed to see how much spiritual growth I had yet to do. I was young in my faith, lacking the spiritual wisdom to make the hard choices. So, I repeated my patterns. I turned my wounds into armor—convinced that vulnerability would only lead to more pain. And yet... there were still those who saw past the walls. Who refused to judge the struggle. Who believed in the story that hadn't even been written yet. To those—who stood by, who never gave up—Thank you.

We can't afford to live in regret. We must not give the enemy the power to drag our past before us—forcing us to relive our failures. Too often, when we look around, we see only what we've done wrong. We allow the world to define our worth— questioning whether we are good enough—whether we measure up. But here's the truth: We don't have to "get good" before coming to God. We don't earn His presence with perfection. Let that sink in. We do not get good to get God—we get God…to get good. Read it again: We don't get good to get God—we get God to get good. We need His direction. We need that still, small voice guiding us deeper into relationship with Him. He knows exactly where we are, who we are, and what we're made of. Nothing is hidden from Him. If only we could trust that His plan is greater than our understanding—trust not only in Him but in the people, He places in our lives.

Can we truly grasp the depth of God's unconditional love? The closest human example is the love of a parent—a love that persists through every mistake, every failure, every misstep. A parent doesn't withhold love when expectations fall short. Love is a choice. Even when the one we love seems unlovable, we continue to love. We don't stop loving simply because we no longer feel it. And this—this is a reflection of the love of God. His love surpasses human comprehension, transcending every limitation we place on love. It is a love that doesn't waver—a love that remains, even when we fail to understand it.

As Christians, we can't afford to focus only on another person's flaws. We can't dismiss someone simply because their sin seems too big—or their struggles too deep. Have we picked up a stone in judgment? Or are we willing to extend grace—the kind Jesus did? Yes, maybe they lied. Perhaps they made mistakes. But have we ever paused to ask... Why? Why are they the way they are? We don't always see the depths of a person's pain the way God does. We don't know what they carry. Have we walked a mile in their shoes? Have we prayed for eyes to see them as He sees them? If we did, perhaps we would recognize the child crying out in fear…the single parent overwhelmed by stress…the addict longing for freedom. It is a prayer we must all pray—no matter how long we have walked with God.

True Godly love doesn't get to cherry-pick who is worthy. We don't get to choose who deserves grace. One of the hardest moments in my healing journey came when the very friend who led me to Christ encouraged me to confront my stepfather face-to-face. My immediate reaction was, "No way!" But as I wrestled with the ideal, I realized my emotions were buried behind the curtain of denial. I'd allowed him to steal my joy, my peace. And anger, deep, raw anger, simmered beneath the surface, like a wild animal clawing at the chance to escape. I didn't need to condone the pain he caused, but I had to acknowledge that I'd let those emotions hold me captive.

When I finally faced him, something shifted. Fear turned to sorrow. I didn't fear him anymore—I pitied him. I found myself asking: "What happened in his life that made him become the man he was?" The day I prayed for his soul was the day I found release. Even my biological father couldn't understand. "How could you forgive him after everything?" he asked. I spoke one word: "God." Forgiveness didn't mean approval. It meant surrender. It meant releasing the pain to God and letting Him bring peace. It meant I'd no longer let hatred decide who I became. Because true forgiveness doesn't wish eternal damnation on anyone. Who did Jesus die for—Every soul, even the ones who hurt us. We've all been wounded, but can we pray for the individual who hurt us? Can we pray for their healing or peace? Our human instincts shout, "Absolutely not!" But is that God's way? The peace I found when I surrendered my pain to Him—was beyond words, indescribable. Even as I attended my stepfather's funeral, I prayed, not in anger, not in bitterness. But with quiet hope—hoping that, in his final moments, he had made peace with God. Because the truth is, every soul deserves mercy and grace. That's what Calvary paid for. But the question remains: Do we extend that mercy? Or do we let our judgments decide who is beyond redemption?

It's time to confront the elephant in the room—or remove the frogs from our lives—and admit the obvious: We are human. But by the grace of God, we are more than that. We are more than conquerors: We are the ones God chooses, the ones He wants to use. We are His hands, His voice, and His vessels. And when we finally recognize that we are who we are only because He loved us through our darkest days—then and only then, do we begin to understand what it truly means to love others. That is growth. Growth that, when rooted in God, produces a harvest of souls.

Five: Provision In the Silence

Discovering God's Presence in the Impossible

I have seen prayers answered. Yet often, in my experience, when we receive exactly what we ask for, we unknowingly shortchange ourselves. As scripture reminds us:

> "For my thoughts are not your thoughts, neither are your ways my ways," declares the Lord. "As the heavens are higher than the earth, so are my ways higher than your ways and my thoughts than your thoughts."—Isaiah 55:8-9 NIV

If we're truly honest, most of us already have an idea of how we think God *should* respond. Whether we're praying for healing, direction, or provision, we come with expectations—assumptions about what outcome is best. But in doing so, we limit God. We lessen who we are in Him, evaluating our worth through flawed, human lenses. We become our own worst critics. We convince ourselves we have to be perfect to be used by God—but that kind of thinking isn't scriptural. Over and over, God used the overlooked, the dismissed, the least expected. He spoke through a donkey. He moved through a burning bush. He worked through people the world would never have chosen. And if God could use a donkey, why would we ever doubt He could use us?

Every day, I am reminded: this journey is not about who I am. It's about who *He* is. When God moves through us, the world doesn't see our glory—it sees *His*. But for that to happen, we must first be willing.

There was a time in my life when I was not willing—when the mere thought of physical touch unsettled me. Whether it was a handshake, a hug, an embrace, or even the gentlest kiss, they were all out of the question. My soul recoiled at contact, though I couldn't always admit why. But God saw the inward battle—the silent storm I refused to acknowledge. Raised in an abusive environment, touch had become the enemy—a tool of torment, wielded in secret yet paraded in public humiliation. It was a game to the abuser, but to me, it was a prison. I grew sickened by the thought of affection, shrinking away from even the smallest gesture. What was meant to comfort had become a form of control.

Yet in His infinite grace, God longed to reveal something deeper—that touch, in its purest form, was created to heal and love. Even in prayer, I struggled. When hands were laid on me for healing, fear gripped my body. I trembled, rejecting the act even as I longed—deep down—for the embrace of a mother's love. I believed I was damaged goods, irreparably broken. I pleaded with God to change me. I didn't want to be an outsider, watching others experience what I could not. But no matter how fervently I prayed, I couldn't erase the scars. So, I convinced myself that reaching out wasn't worth the pain. I rationalized my isolation, filtering every moment through a distorted lens. When brokenness is all you've ever known, how else are you to think? But what I didn't realize was that God was preparing to reveal something far greater—what true, godly affection was meant to be.

God is perfect in all His ways—higher and wiser than anything we could comprehend. I never saw the change happening, yet before I knew it, a transformation had begun. After each church service, different ladies would linger to chat, offering a warm handshake or a heartfelt hug. At first, it was difficult—almost unbearable. I smiled outwardly, but inwardly, I shuddered. I thought to myself, *"This is the huggiest church I've ever seen."* Honestly, at first, it aggravated me. There was no escaping the efforts. I'd dodge one sister's embrace, only to find myself stumbling into the open arms of another. Eventually, it became clear that resistance was futile. I reluctantly settled into the reality of what was happening—whether I liked it or not. Service after service, the parade of hugs continued. And then…something unexpected happened. Over time, I found myself relaxing. The walls I had built began to weaken, and the embraces—once so foreign and unwelcome—slowly became familiar. I started to accept them as more than just gestures. They were expressions of Godly affection, carrying no harm, no hidden motives—only love. And instead of recoiling, I began to recognize something sacred in them—something healing. Of course, I'd never admit that... not out loud. But evidently, God has a sense of humor.

Eventually, I not only found comfort in these embraces—I began to expect them. But just when I thought I had come to terms with it all, something shifted again. As different ones hugged me, I would suddenly feel a kiss on the cheek. *Wait. What was happening now?* It was as if they sensed my lingering reluctance and were gently nudging past it. Again, I struggled inwardly, though outwardly, I smiled—because I couldn't let it show that they were getting to me. But deep down, I knew they were.

It would take years before I truly understood the ministry of embrace. I was speaking at a Women's Conference in Louisiana, stepping further into the journey of healing, when I encountered something unexpected. A ministry unlike any I had known. As I knelt at the altar, praying with different women, a stranger approached. Without hesitation, she wrapped her arms around me, holding me close—firm yet gentle, unwavering yet tender. I was startled by her boldness, my mind racing to process the sudden embrace. But in that moment, something happened. It was different. It was warm. It was steady. And in that sacred pause, thought itself slipped away as I felt something beyond the physical—a supernatural embrace that seemed to radiate straight from the heart of God Himself. It was as if heaven had reached down and cradled me in a love I had never understood. Without warning, the floodgates burst open. Tears—hot and unrestrained—poured freely. My body trembled, overwhelmed by a release I hadn't anticipated. Deep within, emotions long buried clawed their way to the surface—feelings I had silenced, wounds I had numbed. For years, they had lain dormant, hidden behind walls I'd built for protection. But now, they surged forward, refusing to be ignored for one more moment.

Sensing my struggle, the kind stranger whispered, "It's okay, let it go." Her voice carried a peace foreign to me—yet somehow, it settled deep within, steady and sure. I tried to speak, fumbling through sobs to offer an apology. But she shook her head, offering a smile. "No need to apologize," she said. "God wanted you to feel His embrace." *His* embrace? The words settled into me like revelation. *God's* embrace? I had never thought of it that way. I never imagined that such love could be felt in something so simple, so human—so Holy. Intrigued, I accepted her invitation to sit with her for lunch. The questions tumbled from my lips faster than I could contain them. How could an embrace minister so deeply? Why was it so important? How could a mere stranger affect my life in such a profound way? I needed to understand—I wanted to know everything there was to know about this healing hug.

What I failed to realize was that this wasn't the first healing hug I had experienced—but it was the first one I had truly let in.

69

It was a breakthrough, another step along the winding path of restoration that God had carefully laid before me. Little by little, He had been preparing me, using the women in my church as vessels of gentle persistence. What I didn't understand—yet— was that He had placed it on a friend's heart to embrace me...to help me unlearn the fear I had carried for so long. She felt my resistance—sensed the quiet retreat in my spirit—and was led to send others in her place. This was no accident. This was divine strategy. She, too, carried a ministry of healing through embrace—a touch that didn't demand but invited, that didn't take but gave. Feeling the deep hesitation within me, she pressed forward—not in force, but in faith. And when she saw that I was beginning to soften, she encouraged the women to go further... to extend their affection beyond an embrace—to a simple, tender kiss on the cheek.

At the time, I had no understanding of the depth of healing happening within me. I hadn't chosen this approach. If given the option, I would have never chosen this as my path to recovery. But God—whose wisdom far surpasses human reasoning—knew exactly what I needed. He saw wounds buried so deep that even I had forgotten them. And so, He sent a friend—carrying not just comfort, but a divinely detailed plan for healing that reached places in my soul I never imagined possible. It was yet another answered prayer—one I had never even realized I had prayed.

If only we fully grasped the ministries God intends, how intricate, how deliberate—they would shake the very foundations of our churches. They would draw the lost, the broken, the searching—not with spectacle, but with the undeniable presence of divine love in action. At times, I wonder if we truly recognize when our prayers have been answered. Not just answered—but fulfilled down to the smallest detail.

I remember such an answered prayer early in my marriage. One morning, my husband, Wayne, woke to get ready for work, but something was different. I sensed it immediately. Wayne, who was normally lighthearted, quick to tease and fill our home with laughter, moved differently that day. His steps were slow— heavy with an unseen weight. His prayers, usually vibrant and full of gratitude, felt distant... routine, rather than heartfelt. "What's wrong, honey?" I asked. "Nothing," he mumbled. But I knew better. I pressed again, gently but firmly. "I know when something's wrong. Tell me." The year had been grueling. Our youngest son, Tyler, had spent months in the Children's Hospital—surgery after surgery, setback after setback. His health had become a daily battle that drained not only our strength but also our finances. We struggled to stay afloat, scraping together enough to cover the essentials. To help offset the cost of groceries, we planted a garden—praying it would stretch our budget. God blessed our efforts abundantly. Vegetables grew in abundance, spilling over in generosity. I canned them, prepared meals, and shared the overflow with others. Wayne never once complained. He was thankful. But that morning, discouragement crept into his voice. "I'm thankful for all the vegetables," he sighed. "But a man needs his meat." He scoffed, grabbed his things, and walked out the door—completely unaware that God had already heard his unspoken prayer.

The morning unfolded in its usual rhythm—at least, as normal as life could feel during uncertain times. Realizing the time, I rushed into the children's rooms, nudging them awake with gentle persistence. The school bus would be arriving soon, and I didn't want them to miss it. Still wrapped in sleep, they stirred slowly, their grogginess evident. But I urged them forward, reminding them of breakfast and our cherished time of prayer.

As they settled in the living room for prayer, my mind drifted back to Wayne's earlier words. "A man needs his meat." It was a statement drenched in longing. And I understood why. I understood the weight of it, the quiet ache beneath the remark. There was no extra money in the budget for food, let alone meat. With time slipping away, I whispered a quiet, desperate prayer, *"Lord, we need You to provide."*

The low rumble of the approaching bus cut through my thoughts. Our prayer time was brief but heartfelt. The children gathered their backpacks, exchanged quick hugs and goodbyes, and dashed down the driveway to board. I watched them disappear onto the bus, then turned back toward the house, bracing myself for the day ahead. There was much to do—chores waiting, tasks piling up—but the heaviness in my heart lingered. I had learned through experience that if I didn't surrender my burdens to the Lord, they would consume me, making the simplest tasks feel impossible. So, I returned to my quiet place, kneeled, and cried out to Him. *"Encourage Wayne, Lord.*

Strengthen him. Bless his day." The words spilled from my soul with raw urgency.

And then—out of nowhere—a knock at the door. The sound jolted me. I hesitated. Who would be knocking this early? Peeking through the front door curtains, my breath caught. Two men in sunglasses stood on the porch. My heart pounded. Bill collectors? Had they come to collect on a debt we couldn't pay? I grabbed the phone and quickly dialed my mother-in-law, who lived next door. "Can you come over right away?" I whispered. Hanging up, I cautiously spoke through the door. "Can I help you?" One of the men responded, "Can you step outside?" Just then, I saw my mother-in-law approaching through the front gate. Relief washed over me. Feeling secure, I opened the door. "Yes," I said, stepping out. The men gestured for me to follow. Heart pounding, I walked with them toward the fence at the edge of our yard. And then—I saw it. My steps faltered. Hanging from the fence by its hooves was a deer. The men explained that as they were driving by, they saw it sprint across the road and try to leap the fence. But in a cruel twist of fate, its legs caught the wire, causing it to fall and break its neck, instantly. Now, it hung suspended right where it had fallen, lifeless and still. One of the men turned to me and asked, "Can we have it?" I rubbed my eyes, stunned. "No..." I said slowly, still trying to process what I was seeing. "It's okay. We'll keep it."

As the men drove away, my father-in-law pulled into the driveway. What I didn't realize was my mother-in-law had called him, sensing we might need help. Relief flooded me, I realized I needed assistance to move the deer, pulling it down off the fence and placing it onto the old engine puller in the backyard. As we worked together, dragging the deer around the house, my father-in-law smirked and asked, "Sis, have you been praying again?" Puzzled by his question, I looked up. "Yes, sir." His grin deepened. "Did you pray for meat?" My breath caught. I had! Mere moments ago, I had asked God to provide. Never— never—had I expected Him to answer in this way, this quickly, this directly. "Yes!" I exclaimed, laughter bubbling up with the shock of it all. He chuckled, shaking his head. "Well, next time, can you pray that it comes packaged?" I looked at the deer, then up toward heaven, my heart overwhelmed. God had heard. God had answered. Right down to the smallest detail. And if you're wondering whether we had deer meat for dinner that night? Oh, yes. Of course we did.

"Are not two sparrows sold for a penny? Yet not one of them will fall to the ground outside your Father's care. And even the very hairs of your head are all numbered. So don't be afraid; you are worth more than many sparrows."—Matt 10:29-31 NIV

How easily we forget that the God who spoke the universe into existence also bends low to hear the whispers of His children. We convince ourselves that our needs—our quiet desires—are too small, too trivial to warrant His attention. The enemy whispers lies, sowing doubt into the fabric of our faith. *Does God really care about something as simple as this?* Scripture says yes. Our every longing, spoken or unspoken, matters to Him.

My husband, Wayne, was a faithful man—one who carried unwavering trust in the Lord. But even the faithful grow weary. Even the strong have moments of discouragement. His remark that morning, *"A man needs his meat"* was not a complaint, but a sigh of longing. And though it seemed insignificant in the grand scope of life, it mattered to God. He didn't just hear the prayer I whispered that morning. He heard the deep yearning of Wayne's heart; the quiet sigh wrapped within his words. And in a way that only God could orchestrate, He answered—not later, not in some distant future—but *immediately*, sending provision straight to our front yard. It wasn't just meat for dinner. It was a love letter from heaven. A message written in grace and hung by its hooves in our front yard:

I see you. I know what you need. I care. Every time we sat at the table and cut into that venison—every time we prepared it, seasoned it, gave thanks for it—it echoed through our home like a sacred melody: God sees. God knows. God provides.

Not always the way we expect, not always the way we ask, but always in ways that reveal His infinite love and attention to detail. And if we could truly grasp that, if we could understand the depth of His care—not just in the miraculous, but in the everyday—we would never again doubt His presence in our lives.

Have we forgotten that our steps are ordered by God? That He is sovereign over every moment, every challenge, every tear we shed? Too often, when trials come, fear takes hold. We wrestle with uncertainty, questioning whether God truly has a plan amidst the struggle. Yet, if we could only step back—if we could see with eyes of faith—we would realize every hardship, every delay, every *unanswered* prayer is intricately woven into a divine tapestry far greater than we can comprehend. God doesn't send trials to break us—He allows them to build us, to teach us, to refine our trust in His perfect will. If only we would hold steady and not detour the path He has set before us.

This truth became real to me in yet another answered prayer. Wayne and I were both working, pouring every ounce of effort into providing for our family. Yet, no matter how disciplined we were, no matter how carefully we stretched each dollar, we still found ourselves struggling. We remained faithful in our tithes and offerings, clinging to the promise that God would sustain us. But some days felt impossibly heavy. Every meal required creativity—improvising with what little we had. And somehow, despite the missing ingredients, dinner always came together. Until one day—it didn't. There was no way around it. The pantry was empty, the cabinets were bare, and this time, no amount of resourcefulness could change that reality.

Sensing the burden pressing on my shoulders, Wayne asked, "What's wrong, honey?" I sighed. My voice was quiet, but final. "It's over. There's nothing left. I can't make dinner." Wayne listened, and then calmly responded, "God will provide." I stared at him, searching his face for any flicker of doubt—but there was none. How could he rest in faith so easily? Didn't he see how desperate the situation had become? I wasn't worried for myself;

76

I knew we could manage skipping a meal. Truthfully, already had sacrificed—missing lunches at work, skipping dinners to ensure our children had enough. We told them we were "fasting", masking the reality behind spiritual words. But this time—there was nothing. I rummaged through the cabinets one last time, praying for some forgotten ingredients to appear, but they remained stubbornly empty.

Then, the phone rang. It was a dear friend—a missionary serving in another country. Her voice carried urgency. "You've been on my heart all day," she said. "I felt led to call. Is everything okay?" I hesitated. How could I admit the truth? I was ashamed it had gotten this bad. I assured her everything was fine, but she wasn't convinced. Gently, she pressed further, and finally, the truth spilled out. She listened—kindly, without judgment—and offered encouragement. *"Trust Him,"* she urged. *"God will provide."* Her words brought a moment of comfort, but as I hung up, reality remained—*What about dinner?* Then—another interruption. A knock at the back door. Wayne and I exchanged glances. My heart raced. Who would be knocking this late? Peering out the window, I saw our neighbors—an elderly couple who had always been like grandparents to our children. But something was different. Their faces were serious. Concern filled their eyes. "We need to talk," they said gently. "In private." Panic stirred inside me. Our secret was out. These were the parents of the friend who had just called. And now—standing in our doorway—they held the answer to the very prayer we had barely dared to voice. Her father turned to Wayne and said firmly, "Put your shoes on. You're coming with me." Wayne obeyed without hesitation, quietly following him out the door and into the night. He didn't ask questions. He didn't argue. He just went. While they were gone, our neighbor's mother turned to me, her gaze steady. "You have to learn to ask for help," she said. I looked down, ashamed. *"We love you."* She continued. "And when there is a need, pride must never keep you from receiving. The family of God takes care of one another. If the roles were reversed, wouldn't you want to help?" Her words pierced through every wall I had built. She was right. Pride had tried to keep me quiet. But receiving help—it wasn't weakness. It was trust. It was humility. It was love. I would later learn Wayne had received the same speech. But in that moment, something shifted—not just in provision, but in understanding. This was more than groceries. It was an opportunity to receive tough love—offered with wisdom, spoken with grace. From that night forward, they weren't just neighbors. They became family.

Their encouragement shaped our journey. Her husband became a constant source of motivation for Wayne—pushing him to believe in himself, to step boldly into the calling God had placed on his life. *"They need you,"* he would say. "You're called to something bigger. Don't be afraid to go for it." His words weren't just inspiration—they were confirmation. He saw something in Wayne that others had missed. And when he passed away, it left a void we still feel to this day. But his voice? His legacy? It still echoes. It still drives us. And his wife? She remains one of my most treasured confidantes. Sometimes, it feels as if she *senses* things—always knowing when I need support, when a timely word of reassurance is needed. She's the one who watches our home when we travel, gathers our mail, tends to the little things without being asked. I wouldn't trade her for any other neighbor. She doesn't just live next door—she stands beside us. God knew. He knew we needed them. He knew the strength they carried, the encouragement they would bring. Long before we ever saw it—He had already woven them into the story. They weren't a coincidence. They were provision. They were part of His plan all along.

Struggles seemed to weave themselves into the fabric of our lives, appearing when we least expected them and stretching us beyond what we thought we could endure. During one of those difficult seasons, winter arrived with a vengeance. A thick layer of snow blanketed the ground, trapping everything beneath its icy grip. It was the kind of storm that silenced the world—forcing life into stillness. Our neighbors—our steady source of encouragement—were out of town. The roads were slick, treacherous, isolating us from the familiar help we had come to rely on. Inside, I paced the kitchen, searching for something—anything—to create a meal. But there was nothing left. No clever substitutions, no scraps to stretch. Just empty cabinets and the weight of desperation pressing down on my spirit. Then—suddenly—a knock at the door. I froze. Who could possibly be out in this storm? Opening the door, I found a dear friend from church standing there, bundled tightly against the bitter cold, her breath forming clouds in the frigid air. She offered a quick apology, explaining she had meant to stop by sooner—but life had kept her busy. I shook my head in disbelief. "Why are you out in this weather? It's not safe." Her response was simple, yet

79

it carried the undeniable weight of heaven. "God spoke," she said, "and I knew I had to come right away." Without hesitation, she handed me two small bags of groceries—then, just as quickly, hurried off into the storm. Wayne walked into the room, rubbing the sleep from his eyes. *"Who was that?"* he asked, surprised that anyone would brave the icy conditions. I recounted what had happened, and as understanding settled in, he smiled and said, *"God still provides."* I nodded, grateful even for a few groceries. It would be enough for a meal or two. But when I opened the bags, my breath caught in my throat. Tears welled up in my eyes, and before I could stop them, they spilled over in uncontrollable sobs. Because tucked between the groceries was something I never expected—something that left me trembling in the overwhelming presence of God's love: A five-hundred-dollar gift card to our local grocery store. How did she know? How could she possibly have known the depth of our need—the severity of our struggle? The answer was simple. She didn't. But God did. And He had spoken. She had listened. And once again, He had answered. There's something profoundly beautiful about prayer. Jesus answers. Not always in the way we expect, not always in the way we ask—but He answers.

Too often, we view answered prayers as mere responses to a request, forgetting what they truly are—building blocks of faith, whispers of divine intimacy, proof that God is nearby. With every answer, God invites us closer. With every provision, He reveals more of Himself. And with every moment of miraculous timing, our trust deepens. Wayne and I didn't realize it at the time, but every moment of provision, every unexpected miracle,

80

was forming a *yes*—a confirmation of the calling God had placed upon our lives. And when the moment arrived—the moment where faith would be required on a whole new level—would we be ready?

Trials felt like a constant thread woven into the fabric of our lives. They came in waves—relentless and unyielding. People often remarked that our family mirrored the trials of Job: hardship after hardship, yet somehow, we held onto faith—even when understanding felt just out of reach. We knew God was working. But sometimes, His plan felt like a puzzle with too many missing pieces—pieces we desperately longed to find.

Wayne had endured years of back pain, but on one particular afternoon, everything changed. I received an urgent call: He couldn't walk. The pain had become unbearable. I rushed to pick him up from work and drove straight to the hospital. The news was devastating, the damage was crippling, and immediate surgery was his only hope for relief. We returned home to prepare and wait for the surgeon's call, trusting—again—that God had a plan, even if we couldn't see it.

But the very next day, I had a doctor's appointment. I, too, had battled pain—deep, unrelenting pain in my stomach that refused to subside. After several tests, the doctor returned, her expression grave. The pain she explained was caused by a tumor pressing against several organs. It was larger than expected, more aggressive than anticipated. Surgery was urgent. Her words hit like a brick wall. I shook my head. No, I wouldn't schedule surgery—not yet, I had to talk to Wayne. He was already facing his own crisis. How could we both have surgery at the same time? My heart was panicked, fearful of the days ahead.

When I arrived home, Wayne immediately noticed something was wrong. My face was flushed; my movements strained. Not wanting to alarm the children, I asked to speak to him in private. As soon as we stepped into the bedroom, the weight of the news overwhelmed me. I collapsed into Wayne's arms, sobbing. "The news isn't good," I whispered, the words barely escaping my lips. Wayne didn't flinch. He pulled me closer, his voice steady. "Whatever it is, we will get through it." I shook my head, tears spilling. "I can't. I can't have surgery. It's impossible for both of us to go through this at the same time." Wayne listened, absorbing every detail as I struggled to explain. Then, his response was simple, unwavering. "It's going to be okay. Schedule the surgery."

Within the week, both surgeries were completed. Recovery was slow, but grace met us in the form of kindness. Women from the church stepped in like angels—cooking meals, helping clean, filling in the gaps where we simply couldn't. They carried the weight we couldn't lift. For a moment, it felt like we were finally on the road to healing. But then—the unexpected. A few months later, I returned to the doctor, believing the worst was behind me. I was wrong. The tumor had returned. It was growing rapidly, more aggressively than before. And now—chemotherapy was my only option. Frustration surged through me. Hadn't we endured enough? Hadn't we been faithful? I wrestled with God, struggling to understand the purpose of this new trial. But whether I wanted to face it or not, there was only one way forward—head-on. And once again, God moved. He sent new people into my life—people willing to drive me to appointments, sit with me during treatments, hold my hand when the nausea hit, and clean up when I couldn't. They were more than friends. They were *angels*.

Angels who stepped into my pain with compassion, who helped carry the unbearable, who spoke strength when I had none. They ministered, supported, encouraged—and sometimes even provided financial help when we were too overwhelmed to ask for it.

In that season, I came to a life-altering realization: these weren't just kindhearted individuals crossing my path. They were pieces of a greater puzzle, placed by God. Each one was part of a bigger picture I couldn't yet see. Together they formed something rare—a *family*. A family not bound by blood but forged in faith. A special family. God's family.

And when we thought life was improving disaster struck again. Without warning, my job decided they no longer wanted to deal with my health insurance complications. And just like that—without hesitation, without consideration—they let me go. Ten years of unwavering dedication. Ten years of arriving first, staying late, working beyond what was required. Ten years of loyalty—dismissed like an afterthought. I had given everything to this company, poured myself into my work, sacrificed time, energy and worse yet family moments. And when difficulties arose, their decision was swift and cold. I wasn't worth the trouble. I wasn't worth the fight. *"Okay, Lord...get the glory out of this,"* I muttered through gritted teeth, trying to muster faith through the sting of betrayal. But the reality was devastating. What would we do without insurance?

My chemotherapy treatments alone cost six hundred dollars each—not including the additional doctor's expenses. The numbers weren't just intimidating. They were impossible. Then—came a miracle I didn't see coming. To my complete shock, my doctor agreed to administer the treatments *for free*—if I could cover the cost of the medication. His generosity stunned me. It was more than I had hoped for. But even as I left his office that day, one harsh truth lingered: I didn't have the money. Yet, even in the uncertainty, I had learned one thing—God is faithful.

And faithful He proved to be. With each treatment, the exact amount—six hundred dollars—arrived. Not from a known source. Not from someone aware of my situation. But from different individuals—each moved by something they couldn't explain, each feeling led to give *exactly* what was needed. Time after time, God provided. Until finally, the drug company approved sending the medicine for free. God hadn't abandoned me. He had carried us through every roadblock, every closed door, every painful season. And through it all, something had begun to shift inside me. The eyes of my heart were opening, learning to see beyond the struggle—learning to recognize *God in the midst of it.* Not just in the grand miracles, but in the quiet provisions. Not just in the victories, but in the battles fought in unseen places. Like Job at the end of his journey, I now speak faith to you, the reader of this story. One day, you will be able to say,

"My ears had heard of you but now my eyes have seen you."
Job 42:5 NIV

Job had spent his life believing in God—but he hadn't truly *seen* Him. Not *until* the trials came. Not *until* he walked through the fire. Not *until* he had trusted even in his pain—even when everything around him seemed to crumble. And when he emerged on the other side, his faith was no longer secondhand. It wasn't just something he had heard about, it wasn't just a story passed down by his parents or whispered in prayer. It wasn't just a belief built from tradition. It was real. It was personal. It was his own... *"Mine eye seeth thee."*

That's when I saw Him too. Not in the easy seasons. Not when life was neatly tied up in a bow. But when the trials stripped everything away—my security, my certainty, my control—I saw a God who embraced me. A God who didn't walk away when things got messy. A God who carried me when I couldn't carry myself. I realized then—my life wasn't meant to be wasted. It wasn't meant to be *poured out*. It was meant to strengthen others; meant to serve a greater purpose I couldn't fully see just yet. A purpose that would be revealed... if I was willing to walk in His calling.

So, I ask you—Do you want to see God? Do you want to know Him? Because to see or know Him isn't just about familiarity. It isn't head knowledge or surface religion. It's intimacy—it's trust—it's relationship. it's saying, "Even if I don't understand, I trust You." Even if the storm rages. Even if the mountain won't move. Even if the prayer isn't answered the way I hoped. It's saying, "I trust You anyway." If you are willing to believe like Job did—if you are willing to *trust through the pain* and *lean into the unknown*—Then one day, you too will whisper, *"God, I see You!"*

If you are standing in brokenness, asking, *"Can I see God in my pain?"* *"Can I find hope in this situation?"* *"Is God's love really for me?"* I want to shout YES! Yes, a thousand times over. But I can't answer these questions *for* you. You must find them for yourself. You must take the step. You must trust. And when you do—when you surrender the uncertainty, when you lay down the weight of every unanswered question—You'll discover something life-changing. Answered prayer isn't just about solutions. It's about *seeing God*—in the very place where you once believed He was absent. It's about realizing that *He never left at all.*

Six: The Beauty of The Scar

Where Pain Meets Purpose

*L*ife finally began to embrace a rhythm of divine purpose as we settled into our walk with the Lord. The turbulence of our past quieted, allowing a beautiful sense of normalcy to take root. We poured our hearts into the ministry, feeling the unshakable joy that comes from serving. The church we found felt like home—warm, accepting, and unwavering in its embrace. We belonged. We thrived. Our children, once hesitant, found their footing too—growing in faith and forming bonds in the youth group. It was as if every missing piece had finally fallen into place. And for the first time in what felt like forever, we exhaled... basking in the grace of stability. Our passion for Children's Ministry had flourished. Together, we designed elaborate set pieces, crafted fresh adventures, and witnessed the wide-eyed wonder unfold in the hearts of young believers. It was more than a calling—it was a dream realized. The energy was electric, the passion contagious, and every moment felt rich with purpose. But beyond the lessons and laughter, we found something even more precious: community. We didn't just serve—we belonged. We forged friendships that went deeper than surface smiles. We laughed until we cried, celebrated victories big and small, and leaned on one another when life got hard. This church felt eternal—like our "forever place." Ministry wasn't a job; it was a joy.

Yet, something unexpected began to stir. It was subtle at first—a whisper, a shift, a quiet nudge in the depths of our spirits. A sense that something was changing beneath the surface of our perfectly planted lives. There had been no offense, no wounds, no falling out. Just a quiet stirring that neither of us could ignore. Wayne and I began having private conversations, late into the night. We prayed. We questioned. We searched for answers. Why did we feel this way when everything seemed right? Why did we sense God calling us away from the place that had brought us so much fulfillment and peace?

After months of wrestling with uncertainty, we realized we couldn't carry the weight of the unknown any longer. We had to speak with Pastor directly. Perhaps he could decipher the inexplicable unrest swirling in our souls. Anxiety gripped us as we laid our hearts bare before him, hoping we wouldn't seem ungrateful or weak. But his response was immediate and unwavering. "I knew this day was coming," he said, a knowing smile tugging at the corners of his mouth. "I've felt it for a few years now, but I struggled with it myself." His words stopped us cold. *Felt it for years?* What did he mean? Before we could voice our confusion, he continued. It was time. Time to expand. Time to reach further than we had ever dared. God wasn't pulling us away—He was calling us higher.

And then Pastor revealed a vision we had never considered before: *Evangelism*. Not a departure from ministry, but a shifting. A shift from local Children's Ministry to evangelizing far beyond the walls we had come to love. We weren't being asked to stop—we were being asked to step out. Then Pastor shared his heart: God was leading us from the local Children's Ministry into full-time Evangelism. He told us the world needed the fire we carried, the passion that had already transformed countless young lives. "It's time to take what you've done here," he said gently, "and carry it to the world." His words hung heavily in the air. Surely not us. We were children's ministers, not evangelists. We belonged in classrooms, in children's church, among wide-eyed kids bursting with faith. Pastor reassured us—we were *exactly* who God had chosen for this calling.

As if on cue, our assistant pastor entered the office with yet another divine opportunity. "Brother Red has an offer for you," Pastor said. The Holiday Youth Convention in Nashville, Tennessee needed a Children's Evangelist that very weekend. Just like that, an open door appeared—one that would take us beyond everything we'd ever known. An invitation to step beyond the boundaries of familiarity. The moment felt surreal. We froze. Fear clawed at our confidence. *Who were we to travel?* Yet, as we hesitantly agreed, a quiet certainty settled into our spirits. God was moving. He was making a way.

That weekend in Nashville shattered every hesitation. The atmosphere was electric; each service was power packed. We stood in awe, watching God work beyond anything we had ever imagined. Pastors and directors approached, invitations came in, doors swung open. And in that moment, *God's Handywork* was born.

The ministry grew, stretching beyond weekends, beyond our vacation days, beyond what we had ever envisioned. We soon traveled across the United States and into Canada, witnessing firsthand the power of God's hand in every service. Our calendars overflowed. Churches and events lined up, yet we simply couldn't meet every request. We drove through the night, sacrificed sleep, and juggled full-time jobs with relentless travel. Exhaustion crept in, undeniably draining, yet we refused to slow down. We *knew* we were in the will of God, but our bodies bore the weight of the sacrifice. Then, after deep prayer and fasting, Wayne voiced what had been lingering in his heart. "I think we need to go full time," he said, his voice steady. "Are we working for man—or are we working for God?" The question hung heavily in the air. Full-time ministry meant surrendering security—our jobs, our insurance, our stability and worse yet, our safety net. It meant stepping away from everything secure and placing all our trust in the One who had called us.

But as we reflected on our journey, the answer became clear. Every hardship we had endured, every unexpected twist, every painful loss had prepared us for this moment. My own job loss had been no accident—it was preparation.

Every step, even the painful ones, had led us to this moment. And so, with trembling hands but steady hearts, we said yes. We walked away from what the world called security and stepped into the unknown—into a full-time Children's Ministry with a vision to reach the whole world.

Looking back, we now see how every step—every trial and every triumph—was divinely orchestrated, preparing us for this moment in our lives. It was as if the final puzzle piece had slipped seamlessly into place, revealing a breathtaking masterpiece that had been there all along, painted by the hand of God. The path that once felt fragmented and uncertain suddenly made perfect sense. Every challenge we faced, every heartbreak we endured, and every sacrifice we made had become brushstrokes in His greater design, setting in motion a ministry forged through fire. And yet, we hadn't seen it before.

Was it the weight of our struggles that clouded our vision? The sting of loss? The grip of fear? Maybe we were just so caught up in surviving that we forgot to look for the purpose in the pain. But now—on the other side of clarity—we saw it all. His fingerprints were on everything. He had guided each step, not with cruelty, but with a loving, intentional hand.

Though excitement filled our hearts and faith propelled us forward, we had not fully grasped the depth of the sacrifice required. The calling wasn't just an invitation—it was an altar. Full-time ministry required leaving behind the familiar embrace of our local church. It meant, in time, releasing our children into their own destinies, watching as they stepped away from the ministry team, one by one. Each goodbye carried the ache of a heart torn between love and obedience. It was as though pieces of our souls departed with them, yet in our sorrow, we found solace in knowing they, too, had a divine purpose to fulfill.

Even in moments of grief, our faith whispered the truth— God was the author of this journey, and we would trust Him completely. Life on the road wasn't what we had envisioned. There were moments of loneliness, moments where we longed for the familiar voices and routines we left behind. Saying goodbye to the support system felt like stepping into the great unknown—untethered and unsure. But what we didn't anticipate were the incredible people God would place along the way— friends who would become family, kindred spirits who would walk beside us, voices of wisdom that would shape and uplift us.

Ministry didn't mean we had to walk alone; rather, it meant God would extend our family in ways beyond our imagination. He was weaving a new kind of family—a network of hearts linked not by blood, but by divine appointments. People who believed in the mission, who carried us in prayer, who made room for us at their tables and in their lives. Some friendships are fleeting. But others—like the ones God began forming during this season—were clearly orchestrated by Him. Not accidents. Not coincidences. Just His way of reminding us that no matter where we go, we are never outside the reach of His love.

One such family was the Weeks, who became more than friends; they became a cornerstone of love and support in our journey. Through them, we learned an invaluable truth—that family isn't merely defined by blood, but by the unwavering love, sacrifice, and encouragement that mirrors God's heart. Sometimes, it's about who shows up.

One weekend, while I was recovering from surgery and unable to travel, Wayne called with distressing news—he and our youngest daughter was stranded, desperately searching for a garage to repair the truck. I couldn't go to them, couldn't offer much comfort besides prayer—but I knew I had to do something. Wayne, worn out and frustrated, hadn't eaten, and as a diabetic, that alarmed me.

As concern gripped me, a thought sparked—a quiet reminder from God. The Weeks were nearby. Could they help? With trembling hands, I dialed their number, praying they would answer. The moment Sister Weeks picked up, my fragile composure shattered, and tears spilled over as I struggled to explain the situation. But before I could finish, her voice— steady, reassuring—calmed my racing thoughts. "We'll take care of it," she promised. And true to her word, they did. Not only did they arrange help, but they made sure my family had a warm meal and a hotel room, covered entirely out of their own generosity. A simple act of kindness? Perhaps to some. But to us, it was nothing short of the hands and feet of Jesus, stepping in precisely when we needed it most.

Even now, their love continues to pour into our lives. Their phone calls, texts, and messages come at just the right moments—like whispers from Heaven, reminding us that we are never alone. There have been times when their words were exactly what we needed—piercing through uncertainty, doubt, or weariness. Whether lifting our spirits with laughter, speaking wisdom into difficult decisions, or offering a gentle but firm reminder of God's faithfulness, they always seem to carry the perfect message for the season we're in. I find myself eagerly awaiting the videos Sister Weeks shares. Some days, she has us laughing until our sides ache; other days, her words remind us of the depth of love she and her family hold for us. Their church, too, has become more than a place of ministry—it has become a sanctuary, a second home where we find renewal and peace. There, we are surrounded by hearts that embrace us as family.

Even more beautiful is the bond we have formed with several of the families in their congregation. Some affectionately call us "Mom and Dad", a testament to the deep and special connection God has woven into our time together—whether through ministry, summer camp, or shared moments of joy and growth.

Through it all, one truth remains—family is not just bound by genetics, but by love that reflects the heart of God. In the end, it's not the blood that ties us together, but faith, kindness, and the unwavering devotion that creates something profound. And in the Weeks, we have found exactly that—a family not born from lineage, but formed through the deep, abiding love of Christ.

God is faithful! If there is one undeniable truth that has been etched into my soul, it is this: His faithfulness knows no bounds. It is relentless, unwavering, and intricately woven into every chapter of our lives, often in ways we don't recognize until hindsight reveals God's masterful design. Every moment, every trial, every divine encounter is orchestrated by the greatest Maestro of all time.

And this moment—this revelation—was no exception. It was a conference unlike any other. As scheduled speakers, Wayne and I took the stage each night, pouring into the children with the message God had laid upon our hearts. But during the day, we were simply attendees—soaking in the richness of His presence, eager to be filled before we poured out again. On one such afternoon, as the preacher delivered his message, something unexpected happened. His gaze locked onto mine, his finger extended, and without hesitation, he called me forward. The sanctuary fell silent as I stepped into the middle aisle, my heart pounding in my chest. And then—he spoke. His words carried authority beyond human understanding, cutting straight to the core of my being. He began to recount my suffering—my pain, my battle with a neck injury that had plagued me. He couldn't have known. But God knew. And in that moment, it became undeniably clear—I had never been alone.

Like a flood, memories rushed in, transporting me to the morning that changed everything. Exhaustion clung to me like a heavy veil, the result of long hours spent preparing for the weekend ahead. But ministry never waits, and neither did my growing to-do list. Wayne, ever my source of encouragement, urged me to take my time. "I'll shower before heading out for a haircut," he reassured, gifting me a few precious moments to gather myself before the day took over. Sitting at the edge of the bed, I felt the gentle hum of my bedside fan, the rhythmic breeze offering a fleeting comfort. Instinctively, I stood to turn it off, thinking nothing of the simple action. But in a heartbeat, my world shifted. A crushing force struck me, swift and unforgiving. A deafening crash filled the air—and then, darkness. The next thing I knew, Wayne was standing over me, his face a mixture of worry and shock. I was no longer standing—I was sprawled at his feet, my head covered in blood. The concern in his voice barely registered through the haze. "What happened?" he asked. For the first time in my life, I had no answer. "I don't know," I whispered, confusion clouding my every thought. The last thing I remembered was reaching for the fan. Now, I was on the floor, disoriented, shaken, vulnerable. Wayne knelt beside me, his hands gentle yet urgent. "Let me help you, baby." But the moment I attempted to stand, dizziness struck like a tidal wave, merciless and unrelenting. The room spun wildly, blurring into chaos. "Put me back in bed!" I gasped, gripping his arm for support. As I lay down, a wave of nausea crashed over me, consuming me whole. Wayne dabbed at the blood on my forehead, his voice a steady anchor in the storm. "Rest a few minutes," he urged, his concern etched into every movement.

Though I assured him I was fine, deep within, I knew something was terribly wrong. Although he didn't want to leave, I knew time was short, so I encouraged him to continue the morning plans. He quickly left for his haircut, promising to help me when he returned. But as I lay in that bed, unmoving, reality settled in—any attempt to turn my head sent the room spiraling into uncontrollable chaos, dragging me into its relentless vortex of sickness.

Wayne returned from the barbershop with a growing unease, something deep in his spirit telling him to check on me. The moment he stepped into the room, his expression changed. I could see it written across his face—something was terribly wrong. Evidently, I looked worse than before. I could feel it too, a heaviness deeper than pain—a weariness that reached into my soul. Weak and desperate, the words escaped my lips before I could second-guess them. "I think you'd better call an ambulance," I pleaded. The very thought of it sent a wave of dread through me. I wasn't the type to rush to the hospital for every ailment. But this—this was different. Something inside me screamed for help.

When the EMTs arrived, they quickly assessed the situation and decided to transport me to the local hospital. I was barely holding myself together. My body was fragile, my senses overwhelmed, and I knew that any movement—however slight—would unleash another vicious wave of nausea. "Please!" I begged. "Don't move me without giving me something for the nausea." But they ignored my warning, confident they could handle the situation. Moments later, as they lifted me, their assurance shattered as sickness overtook, spewing in every direction, before they could react. I wanted to apologize, but deep down, I knew—I had warned them.

The ride to the hospital was a blur, a whirlwind of sounds and motion. But one image stayed with me: Wayne, standing at the door, shoulders heavy, eyes filled with tears as he waved goodbye. There was nothing else he could do. He had to move forward, taking our children to our next destination while I was carried away in the opposite direction, toward uncertainty. Even before I arrived at the hospital, Wayne had called our dear friends, the Spears family, trusting they would meet me and offer the support I so desperately needed.

When they arrived, their reaction was immediate—distress and frustration. Their faces fell the moment they saw me, still sitting in my own sickness, trembling, unable to stop the relentless waves of nausea. It was unbearable. The hospital staff had attempted treatments, but nothing worked. My suffering was agonizing, unrelenting. Sister Spears, watching helplessly, couldn't stand by any longer. She pleaded with the nurses to do something—to help clean me, to offer relief. But when her requests fell on deaf ears, she did what only someone with a true servant's heart would do—she stepped in herself. She cleaned me, cared for me, and brought dignity back to a situation that had stripped it away. In that moment, I saw love in action. True ministry does not always come from a pulpit, nor is it wrapped in grand gestures. Sometimes, it is simply a compassionate hand, willing to do what others will not. Sister Spears was an angel in that hospital room, sent by God Himself to remind me that I was seen, still loved and not forgotten.

Days turned into weeks, and confusion clouded every conversation in the hospital halls. No one had answers. My condition remained a mystery. If I lay completely still, I was fine. But the moment I turned my head in either direction, sickness overtook me. The doctors were at a loss, unsure of how to proceed. We were all grasping at straws, desperate for something—anything—that would point us in the right direction. Finally—a breakthrough. The hospital physician called in an ear, nose, and throat specialist. The moment he stepped into my room, I saw it in his eyes—He knew. Within the hour, I had a diagnosis—Benign Paroxysmal Positional Vertigo, BPPV caused by a neck injury. A wave of relief washed over me. At last—an answer. And more importantly—a solution. The specialist treated me right away, placed a neck collar around me, and with calm confidence said, "You'll be better within a month." It sounded simple, but I had learned by then that healing doesn't always come quickly—or easily. In reality, it would be six long months before I was finally able to remove the collar and walk without assistance.

And now—standing in that conference aisle, a year later, listening to the preacher describe every detail of my injury with prophetic precision—I knew with full certainty that God had never once looked away. He had seen me in my weakness, carried me through my uncertainty, and now, He was using His servant to remind me of His omnipresence, His sovereignty, His unshakeable faithfulness. It was not coincidence. It was divine intervention—His hand reaching into my story, revealing that even in the unseen moments, He had been there.

If there is one truth that echoes through every hardship, every valley, every triumph, it is this—God's faithfulness is not merely a promise; it is a certainty. It does not waver. It does not diminish. It does not falter in the face of difficulty. He sees what we cannot. He moves before we even recognize our need. And He orchestrates every moment, every detail, with a purpose far greater than our understanding. Through it all, He remains the steady, loving hand guiding our journey, proving that no trial, no pain, no moment is wasted in His perfect plan.

So, the moment the preacher—a prophet—stood before the congregation and continued to speak about my neck injury, chills ran through me. My breath hitched, my heart pounded, and for a brief second, time seemed to freeze. How could he possibly know? His words weren't vague—they were precise, slicing through the layers of fear I had so carefully buried within me. He spoke of my struggle—the silent terror that gripped me at the thought of the condition returning, the invisible battle that no one else could see but that tormented me daily.

Then, in an act so bold, so unexpected, he moved my neck forward and backward with such force that my hair barrette flew several pews back. A collective gasp rippled through the sanctuary—a sound of shock and awe—but I barely registered it. My body tensed, my mind raced, yet I felt something shifting— not just physically, but spiritually. His words held me captive, reaching into the depths of my soul. He spoke of my hidden battles—the health struggles that had weakened me, the fears that had threatened to consume me. He saw what I had tried to suppress. He exposed what I thought I had concealed. And then, with authority and compassion, he spoke the words I had longed to hear: *"Trust God."*

Then, the prophet called Wayne forward. The room seemed to shift—the atmosphere grew heavier, charged with something unseen yet deeply felt. My breath caught in my throat, and a chill swept through me as anticipation settled deep in my bones. Something was coming, something significant. And what followed shook me to my core. His voice, steady and filled with authority, carried across the sanctuary like a divine decree. He spoke of an impending storm—an attack from the enemy designed to shake the very foundation of our lives. His words were sharp, deliberate, each syllable cutting through the silence. "You will come dangerously close to bankruptcy," he declared. "You will lose every vehicle you own." The weight of the revelation pressed down on me, yet before fear could take root, his tone shifted—firm, unwavering. "But do not worry. A church will provide." A promise. A lifeline in chaos. Even before the storm arrived, provision would be waiting in the wings. But then, his voice grew heavier. The battle would not end with finances—it would reach beyond material loss, stretching into something far more profound. "You will come face to face with death's door," he announced. My pulse quickened. A shudder ran through me, the words settling deep, not just in my mind but in my spirit. "Don't panic," he assured, his voice unshaken. "God will carry you through." *Carry us through?* The phrase echoed within me, both a warning and a promise. There was no doubt—we would walk through darkness. But we would not walk alone. He pressed forward, unveiling what lay ahead. "The days to come will be brutal," he warned. "A battle of the mind. A season of testing unlike anything you've ever known." This wasn't just about physical hardships, but about an all-consuming refinement—a fire meant to purify, a transformation meant to deepen our faith. "But when you have endured," he continued, "God will honor you with a special anointing. His favor will rest upon you."

The room felt different now, as if heaven itself leaned in to listen. I could feel something shifting—not just around me, but within me. This wasn't merely prophecy—it was preparation. A divine forewarning that demanded our unwavering trust. "The trial is coming, but you must stand firm," he urged. "God will be with you in every step, in every storm, through every unknown. You will walk through fire, but you will not be consumed." The words reverberated in my soul, settling like an anchor. Fear had no place here—only faith. This would be a test unlike any before, but it would not be without purpose. It would mold us, refine us, prepare us for the calling ahead. This was more than a

102

declaration—it was an invitation. To trust. To surrender. To step boldly into the unknown, knowing with absolute certainty that we were held by the hands of the Almighty. The road ahead would demand unwavering trust. It would challenge us, stretch us, refine us. It would teach us what it truly meant to rely on God—not just in the good times, but in the hardest moments, in the places where fear threatens to take hold. And when the season passed, we would not emerge the same. We would know Him in ways we never had before. We would walk in a deeper faith, a greater strength, a surrendered trust that would carry us forward into His calling.

That day, standing in the presence of God, listening to the prophecy unfold, I knew—this was more than just a warning. It was a summons. An invitation to trust beyond what we could see, to lean into the unknown with the certainty that we would never walk alone.

Within mere months, the prophet's words came to pass with a force that rattled the very foundations of my faith. I was rushed into emergency surgery to repair a hole that had formed in my ileum—an unexpected medical crisis, but one I assumed would be resolved quickly. However, in the aftermath of the procedure, something went terribly wrong. A silent, creeping infection had invaded my body, spreading through my system unnoticed until it had already taken hold. By the time my home health nurse detected it, the damage had been done. And instead of staying to fight for my recovery, she chose to walk away. She ended my care abruptly, leaving Wayne and me to face the storm alone.

Wayne, seeing the grave condition I was in, pleaded with me to go to the emergency room. But the battle had drained me. The fight was slipping from my spirit, and I no longer had the strength to push forward. Angered, frustrated, and utterly defeated, I simply wanted to close my eyes and let sleep take me—to escape the weight of it all. But Wayne saw what I couldn't. He recognized the danger, the thin line I was teetering on. In desperation, he called a friend from church, someone nearby whom he trusted to talk some sense into me. Together, they pleaded with me to go to the hospital, urgency threading their voices. And in that moment, I faced the sobering truth— death wasn't just near, it was only a breath away.

When we arrived at the emergency room, everything moved at a frantic pace. The doctor, eyes scanning me with practiced precision, wasted no time. He inserted not one, but two IVs, then immediately quarantined the room. Turning to Wayne and me, he spoke carefully, deliberately: "I don't want to alarm you—but you are in critical condition. Had you waited just a couple of hours more, you wouldn't be here." His words settled over me like a chilling wave. I had been standing at the edge of eternity, and I hadn't even realized it.

Days blurred into one another as my condition rapidly declined. Despite the doctors' relentless efforts, the infection refused to break, seeping deeper, attacking major organs, and forcing them to shut down one by one. Then came the boils—a physical manifestation of the sickness raging within, each one bringing waves of unbearable pain. My body was failing. My mind, too, was slipping, caught in a prison of fear and exhaustion. My room was placed under strict quarantine once more, isolating me further. No one could touch me unless they were fully covered, gloves shielding their hands, and masks covering their faces. And as the loneliness crept in, so did despair. I felt untouchable, forgotten—unseen.

One afternoon, drowning beneath the weight of isolation, I pleaded silently with the Lord. My heart cried out—not for medicine, not for another intervention, but simply for His embrace. I needed to know He was still there, that He hadn't abandoned me, that I wasn't alone in the fight. And then, the door opened. A familiar presence stepped inside—a friend from church, a nurse. She saw me, truly saw me. She didn't look at the sickness, didn't let fear dictate her response. She saw my desperation. She saw the silent plea in my eyes. And without hesitation, without protective gear, without a second thought, she reached out. Ignoring protocol, ignoring rules, she wrapped me in an embrace—the very thing I had just begged God for. "The Lord wants you to feel His embrace," she whispered. That was it. The floodgates broke, and tears poured down my face. God had heard me.

In that one act, that single, unexpected moment of human contact, He answered the most desperate prayer of my heart. That nurse became more than a caregiver—she became a lifetime friend, a vessel through which God's love had reached me when I needed it most. And to this day, her hugs still carry the warmth of heaven. Through her obedience, God reminded me: *I see you. I have not forgotten you. You are not alone.*

Meanwhile, our pastor was also burdened. Deeply disturbed by what we were going through, he retreated to his office and cried out to God. He had watched Wayne endure multiple back surgeries. He had seen a tornado tear through our neighborhood, damaging our home. And now he was witnessing me, lying in a hospital bed, barely clinging to life. "Why, Lord?" he prayed. "Why now? Why them?" And in the quiet of that moment, God responded: *"This sickness is not unto death."* A declaration, a divine assurance.

With a renewed conviction, our pastor arrived at the hospital, stepping into our room like a warrior stepping onto a battlefield. His presence brought a weighty peace, and his words carried authority that pierced through the fog of sickness and despair. He encouraged Wayne and me, reminding us that the enemy's attack would not have the final say. Then, in a moment charged with spiritual certainty, he drew a metaphorical line in the sand—a dividing point between suffering and deliverance. He declared that this sickness would end. That the suffering would cease. That God had already spoken, and His word would not return void.

And then, something miraculous happened. Within hours of that declaration, my body responded in a way that defied logic and baffled the medical staff. The infection—the very thing that had waged war against me, threatening to consume me—began to pour from my body. It was undeniable, unexplainable. Doctors, witnessing the impossible unfold before their eyes, admitted they had never seen anything like it. The very source that had sought to destroy me was being expelled, and in its place, healing was taking root. Three days later, I walked out of that hospital with a clean bill of health. Whole—Restored— Healed.

Once again, the prophet's words had come to pass, solidifying the truth that had now been engraved upon my soul: God had been in control from the beginning. Every step, every trial, every battle had been directed by His hand. He had never abandoned us. And as I left that hospital—free from the sickness that once held me captive—I carried with me an unwavering certainty:—no matter what lay ahead, no matter how fierce the battle, His purpose was unfolding. We would walk in it, knowing without a doubt that His hand was upon us.

From the outside looking in, our trials must have seemed merciless, as if God had set His sights on testing us beyond endurance. To many, it appeared unfair—an onslaught of suffering without reprieve. Friends and family rallied, lifting fervent prayers, fasting, pleading for answers from heaven. But days turned into months, and months into years, with no clear resolution in sight. The silence weighed heavily, stretching faith thin. Even among our most steadfast supporters, doubt began to creep in. Few struggled with this silence more than Sister Spears. A warrior in prayer and, a woman refined by hardship, she had weathered storms alongside us—storms that would have

107

unraveled lesser souls. And yet, as she watched our suffering persist without explanation, something inside her broke. She wrestled with frustration, with weariness, with the aching realization that she no longer believed her prayers carried weight. "What's the point?" she lamented one evening, her voice laced with defeat. Her heart, once ablaze with faith, grew dim. She had spent years interceding for our breakthrough, waiting for divine intervention—only to feel as if she were speaking into a void. The frustration settled deep. The hopelessness became suffocating. And somewhere in that space of unspoken grief, she stopped expecting an answer at all. But God is never absent, even when He feels silent. And in time, clarity would come.

Years later, Sister Spears and her husband, Richard, sat before us with eyes glistening from tears held back. There was something different about their posture—something raw, honest, vulnerable. With trembling voices, they admitted the truth that had weighed on their hearts. "We didn't know if God would answer," they confessed. Their words echoed in the space between us, heavy with the residue of a long, silent battle. They had doubted. They had questioned. And now—now they were seeing what they hadn't been able to see before. The trials that once seemed like cruel afflictions now revealed themselves as divine preparation. "We see it now" they said, their voices threaded with emotion. "Look at what God is doing in your lives." The revelation struck deep. This was not random suffering. This was not a purposeless pain. Every trial, every hardship, every attack had been a steppingstone lifting us toward something greater. Our journey was never about endurance alone—it was about transformation. It was about positioning us for Kingdom work far beyond what we could have ever imagined. Every challenge had been an invitation to step deeper into the calling God had written for us. Every heartache had carried purpose. Every battle had paved the way for breakthroughs.

Now, standing on the other side of understanding, Sister Spears and Brother Richard could finally see what they hadn't before. Their doubt gave way to excitement, to renewed faith. No longer mere observers, they wanted to be participants in the work God was doing. Without hesitation, they were among the first to support the vision financially, choosing to invest not just with words, but with action. They became PIKMIs—Partners in Kids Ministry—offering their hands and hearts to the mission.

Over the years, their friendship has been an unwavering force—a pillar of encouragement, a source of strength in times of uncertainty. And how incredible is the divine design of relationships? The beauty of God's tapestry is not merely in individual threads, but in how He weaves them together. Three families—and many more to follow. Three journeys, each distinct, yet bound by the invisible thread of His purpose, forming a support system that would carry us through seasons— through victories, and through valleys.

Sister Spears is one of my "Three Amigos"—a blessing beyond words, a testament to God's precision in placing the right people at the right time. What once felt like unanswered prayers was, in truth, the foundation for something far greater. And now, with hindsight as our witness, we marvel at His masterful orchestration, knowing He had been writing "our" story all along.

Pain... we often shrink from it, resist it, misunderstand it. We see suffering as punishment, hardship as consequence, and trials as chains binding us to the past. Yet what if pain is not a prison, but a passage? What if trials are not meant to bury us but to build us—one heartbreak at a time, one battle at a time, one scar at a time? God doesn't waste pain. It is not arbitrary. It carries a divine purpose. Pain speaks—it whispers of wounds unseen, of heartaches hidden beneath the surface. It signals an inward struggle—a longing for healing. Yet pain is not the enemy. It is the refining fire, the sculptor's chisel, the Potter's hands shaping us into vessels of resilience, wisdom, and grace.

If you allow it, pain becomes the pathway to transformation. It shifts from torment to testimony, from darkness to divine light. The process is not easy, but when surrendered into God's hands, pain becomes an instrument—not of destruction, but of renewal. We flinch at scars. We hide them, cover them, try to erase them. We see them as remnants of battles we wish had never occurred. But let's look at scars differently. What do you see when your eyes trace the nail-scarred hands of Jesus Christ? You don't see weakness. You don't see defeat. You see *love*. You see redemption. You see the proof of a victory that shattered the gates of hell and conquered sin forever.

When Jesus stood before His disciples after the resurrection, how did they recognize Him? *By His scars.* His wounds were not erased—they were glorified. The same hands that had been pierced for our transgressions became the proof of salvation, the testimony of triumph. What about your scars? Do they tell a story of sorrow, loss, regret? Or do they sing a song of overcoming, endurance, and grace? Your scars do not define your brokenness—they proclaim your strength. They are not marks of ruin; they are badges of survival, reminders that you made it through.

Your scars do not whisper failure; they declare *victory*. The enemy thrives on distortion. He wants you to see your scars as shame—proof of your suffering. But God transforms that narrative. *Your scars are proof of a battle won, a valley crossed, a storm endured.* Do not let the enemy's voice be louder than God's truth. Don't let despair rewrite the testimony of your resilience. You have walked through the fire—and you are still standing. You have faced the storm—and emerged stronger. You have carried the weight of sorrow—and found joy on the other side. If scars could speak, they would tell the story of survival. They would whisper of nights spent wrestling with doubt, days burdened with sorrow, and moments of breaking that led to new beginnings. They would proclaim that grace was sufficient, that mercy was unshaken, that God was faithful.

Isaiah declares this promise so powerfully:

"The Spirit of the Sovereign Lord is on me, because the Lord has anointed me to proclaim good news to the poor. He has sent me to bind up the brokenhearted, to proclaim freedom for the captives and release from darkness for the prisoners, to proclaim the year of the Lord's favor and the day of vengeance of our God, to comfort all who mourn, and provide for those who grieve in Zion—to bestow on them a crown of beauty instead of ashes, the oil of joy instead of mourning, and a garment of praise instead of a spirit of despair."—Isaiah 61:1–3 NIV

There is beauty in the scars. Not because the pain itself was beautiful, but because God redeems every wound, every struggle, every tear. Your trials do not have the final say. The past does not write your future. Your scars are not tombstones— they are testimonies. Your hardships, your struggles, your moments of breaking—all of it carries value. Do not let bitterness, regret, or shame cloud the reflection of what God is doing in you. Others will look at your life—will they see anger? Will they see wounds that remain open, unhealed? Or will they see the *power of transformation*, the strength of a heart redeemed, the beauty of healing?

Let your scars become a light in someone else's darkness. Let your testimony be the bridge that carries another soul out of despair to hope. Be the voice of encouragement, the hands of compassion, the living proof that God restores, renews, and redeems. I'm forever grateful for the nail-scarred hands of Jesus.

To me, they speak of love that cannot be measured, grace that cannot be earned, and mercy that never runs dry. They remind me of a sacrifice I didn't deserve and a love I'll never fully comprehend. Calvary stands as proof that you are valuable in the eyes of God. To Jesus, you were worth dying for—and that truth should ignite hope within your soul.

Healing isn't easy. There will be days when you feel like giving up—days when the weight of it all presses so hard against your heart that forward motion feels impossible. But you must keep going. Your story is not over. Your pain does not define you; it refines you. You have walked through trials that should have broken you, yet here you are—Still standing. Still fighting. Still moving forward.

God doesn't just heal; He redeems. He does not simply restore; He transforms. And He is ready to take your scars—not to erase them, but to use them for His glory. Can you trust Him with the wounds, with the pain, with the process? It may not be easy... but it will absolutely be worth it.

The scars tell a story—but you get to decide how the story ends. You can let them mark you with bitterness, or you can let them be etched with purpose. You can bury them beneath shame, or you can lift them up as a banner of survival. You can silence them in fear, or you can allow them to testify of God's power to redeem what once seemed ruined. The choice is yours. But if you're willing, God will take every scar—every painful memory, every battle fought, every wound endured—and turn it into a testimony of grace. Because in the hands of the Master, nothing is wasted... not even the scars.

Seven: Ministry in the Hard Places

Not Today, Devil. Not This One.

*L*ife is a tapestry woven with divine encounters—some
fleeting, others enduring. We often struggle to recognize
the significance of the people who enter and exit our lives,
mistaking their departure for rejection rather than divine
orchestration. Yet, in His wisdom, God places individuals in our
path to shape us, teach us, and ultimately propel us forward.
Some add immeasurable value, but their presence might become
a hindrance if they remain beyond their season. As we grow in
our faith, we come to understand that we, too, are called to be a
source of encouragement—leveraging our experiences to impart
wisdom into the lives we encounter.

One night, early in our ministry, I stood at the altar during a children's service—my hands lifted, my spirit engaged in prayer. The room was alive, the voices of children rose like incense, their sincerity tangible. Yet, amidst the sacred hum of worship, I felt something shift—an unshakable urge to redirect my focus toward the adults scattered among the crowd. It was then that I heard the unmistakable whisper of God: *"You missed her."* Confusion gripped me. *Missed who?* My gaze darted through the sea of faces until it landed on her—alone, withdrawn, a fortress of silence in the farthest corner of the room. She had been unyielding all service, her expression like stone, her presence distant. If I'm honest, she was the last person I wanted to approach. Yet as I studied her, I saw something familiar— something painful. She was me. Years ago, I had been that woman—broken, guarded, unwilling to trust. And just as God had sent someone for me, He was now sending me to her. Obedience was my only option. Still, as I stepped forward, fear crept in like a shadow. *What if she pushed me away? What if she refused prayer? What if my words fell lifeless at her feet?* But this was not about me. I knelt beside her, my voice steady despite the storm inside me. "I feel God wants to speak to you," I said. "May I pray with you?" Her response cut through the air like a blade. "I don't care what you do." For a moment, silence stretched between us. When God leads me, words usually come effortlessly—but this time, there was nothing. *Lord, why did You send me if You're giving me nothing to say?* Still, I pressed forward. "Let's pray first." I took her hands. The moment I began to pray, it happened. A tremble. A shaking. A deep, uncontrollable release. I lifted my eyes—tears streamed down her face, her body wracked with sobs. The floodgates had broken. The walls that held years of pain were crumbling in His presence. Then the words came—not mine, but His. They poured forth like water in a parched desert, flowing directly into the depths of her brokenness. I watched as healing unfolded before me, watched as God rewrote her pain into peace. She clung to me, desperate, her whisper barely audible: *"Thank you."* Her heaviness had lifted, and I knew her heart had shifted. As her spirit found rest, I continued ministering to others, but something lingered—something Holy, something bigger than the moment itself.

The service ended. The chairs emptied. The room fell quiet. As I packed up, looking for my husband, I noticed him speaking with the pastor. They motioned for me to join them. To my surprise, standing with them was the woman from earlier. The pastor turned to me. "What did you say to her during service?" I hesitated. "Whatever God spoke." He studied my face. "Try to recall exactly what you told her." I recounted each word; the memory still fresh in my spirit—it, was new. Generally, when God spoke, once it left my lips, it also left my mind. As I finished, the pastor turned to the woman. "Give it to her." Then, looking back at me, he said, "Open your hand." I obeyed. "She didn't just write what she's about to give you," he continued. "A week ago, she made a copy and placed it in the offering plate." My breath hitched. With trembling fingers, she pressed a crumpled piece of paper into my palm. Slowly, I unfolded it. And there they were—five questions. Questions she had written in desperation, questions she had cried out to God, questions she had begged heaven to answer. And every single one of them— had been answered, in order, that night. I looked up, overwhelmed, and before I could speak, she threw her arms around me, weeping on my shoulder. Through sobs, she pleaded: "Please don't leave. I want to be baptized in Jesus' name. I want you to be here—to witness this." How could I deny this moment? We promised to return to the night service, to witness her transformation. We would rejoice as she stepped into the water, as she surrendered completely, as she rose anew.

Later that night, as we pulled into the parking lot for service, another vehicle followed behind us—a van. It was her. But this time, she wasn't alone. She had brought friends from the women's shelter—women who had seen the transformation in her and longed for the same encounter with God. She was baptized that night, filled with the Holy Ghost, speaking in tongues as she emerged from the water. And then, one by one, her friends followed. Nine women, Nine baptisms, Nine lives forever changed. I don't know where she is today. I don't know where her journey has taken her. But I do know this—God spoke, and He moved. That night changed her life, but it changed mine, too. It was a reminder that when we listen, when we obey, when we surrender completely—God will speak through us.

If I'm completely honest, children's ministry wasn't the calling I had envisioned. It wasn't my first choice—not by a long shot. Don't misunderstand me—I love it now, with every fiber of my being. It has become my heartbeat, my joy, my sacred assignment. But if I had followed my own desires, I would have pursued a ministry dedicated to the broken—the wounded souls in women's shelters, the weary adults lost in the maze of their struggles, those who carry silent burdens too heavy to bear alone.

Yet, why do we confine ministry to rigid labels? Why do we separate what was never meant to be divided? I once failed to see that God wasn't crafting a ministry for children alone—He was shaping something far greater: a ministry with many arms, reaching across ages, circumstances, and histories. Children's ministry is more than what its name suggests.

Through the years, we have witnessed the undeniable hand of God moving among both the young and the young at heart. Adults walk in expecting nothing more than playful antics— perhaps a puppet show, perhaps an afternoon of laughter and innocence. And yes, there is laughter. But laughter is no mere amusement; it is a balm, a Holy medicine poured into weary souls.

"A cheerful heart is good medicine, but a crushed spirit dries up the bones." Proverbs 17:22, NIV

And so, within the walls of what many dismiss as "children's ministry," miracles unfold. We have seen sight restored to the blind, deaf ears opened, felt broken hearts mended, watched marriages resurrect from ruin, and witnessed families drawn back into the embrace of love—all because we were willing to see beyond the label and minister to those still classified, spiritually, as young at heart.

119

But what defines a child? Is it merely age, or something deeper? Some remain childlike well into their forties, fifties, and beyond—not out of reluctance to mature, but because life never gave them the chance to grow in God. Their struggles run deep—fear, doubt, wounds unhealed—shadows from their past that cloud their understanding. And too often, in our eagerness, we push them forward, forcing spiritual maturity before they are ready. Perhaps that is why some in the church remain stagnant, trapped in cycles of immaturity. And if so, we—the body of Christ—must hold ourselves accountable.

People wrestle not only with the brokenness of the world but with the battle within themselves. They recognize their anger, their bitterness, their difficulty in trusting—but for many, that is all they have ever known. *"Raise up a child"*, the Bible instructs. But are we truly raising them, nurturing them, guiding them toward growth? Or are we merely condemning their struggles, dismissing their pain? Some may not reflect their natural age, but rather their spiritual age. They don't need judgment. They need a hand extended in grace, a voice speaking hope, a heart willing to walk alongside them through the struggle.

And in offering that grace, may we never forget our own journey. May we remember the depths from which we ourselves were lifted.

For as 1 Corinthians 6:11 NIV so powerfully reminds us: *"And that is what some of you were. But you were washed, you were sanctified, you were justified in the name of the Lord Jesus Christ and by the Spirit of our God."*

Growth is a deeply personal journey—one that unfolds at different rhythms for each of us. We must resist the urge to measure ourselves against others, for our experiences—the burdens we carry, the wounds we heal—are uniquely ours.

When I first surrendered my heart to the Lord, it was not in perfect peace but in turmoil. Anger consumed me. I wrestled with questions that tore at my soul. *"Why didn't I fight back? Why didn't I do more?"* My own thoughts became a battlefield, and regret threatened to take root. But in His divine mercy, God sent a precious angel to place this scripture before me:

"When I was a child, I talked like a child, I thought like a child, I reasoned like a child. When I became a man, I put the ways of childhood behind me." 1 Corinthians 13:11 NIV

A revelation unfolded within me—how could I have responded with the wisdom of an adult when I was merely a child? The choices I had made, the silence I kept, were not failings but the desperate survival of a heart too young to comprehend the fullness of its circumstances. My abuser convinced me that speaking out would mean losing everything I held dear—that my family would suffer, that I would be blamed and I believed it. Fear has a way of silencing the innocent, wrapping its arms around truth until it is barely visible.

But even as adults, we struggle with spiritual immaturity. Our walks with God are not uniform, and we progress at different paces, sometimes faltering, sometimes questioning. I've found myself frustrated by my own missteps, asking, *"Why did I allow this? Why did I make that choice?"* The weight of knowing better yet still stumbling can feel unbearable. One of my greatest struggles was learning to trust. Life had taught me that people who promised support could, in the end, deliver only harm. Some inflicted wounds under the guise of kindness. Some preyed-on vulnerabilities for their own gain. And some— whether out of selfishness or sheer malice—sought to break me physically, spiritually, and mentally. Even someone I once held close, a friend I believed in, betrayed me out of jealousy. She spun lies, poisoned the minds of those I cherished, and attempted to dismantle God's ministry. What grieved me most was the innocent children who lost the guidance they so desperately needed, left in confusion because of deceit.

It was in that season of accusation and loss that I turned to God with my broken heart. And He spoke: *"Stand still."* The world teaches us to fight when our name is dragged through the mud—to defend ourselves with every ounce of strength we possess. But God revealed something greater. What would be the testimony of my heart? Would I lash out in anger, or would I allow the fruit of my works to speak truth? There will always be those who seek to dismantle what God is building. The enemy is relentless, using every possible avenue to sow destruction. But we must learn to see these attacks for what they truly are—lies, meant to distract, discourage, and weaken our faith. Defending

122

ourselves to the world can sometimes make us appear
vulnerable, but standing firm with God reveals true strength. The
harvest will come, and the fruits of our labor will be undeniable.

In this journey of faith, we must reach a place of absolute
trust—that God will place the right people in our lives, those
who will nurture and uplift us in truth. As I have often said,
some individuals are only meant to walk with us for a season.
Their departure can be painful, but we must recognize the greater
purpose. They are called to new places, to minister to others just
as they once ministered to us. And isn't it easier to release them
with peace, trusting that God directs every detail? That He, in
His infinite wisdom, knows exactly who and what we need? His
plan is flawless, and we can rest in that assurance. We are each
woven with purpose, carrying immense value when we surrender
our hearts to the transformative work of the Lord.

I'll admit, at first, I struggled to see the beauty and
significance of Children's Ministry. Today, I long for churches
to grasp the extraordinary worth of children—not just as the
future of the church, but as vessels of pure faith, as souls in need
of nurturing, healing, and love. Children's ministry, if done
correctly, is a sanctuary for restoration—a garden where seeds of
faith are sown, watered, and brought to life. But I didn't
recognize that until God called us into its sacred depths. Looking
back, I see the masterpiece He was painting, one brushstroke at a
time.

So, if God directs your steps toward an unfamiliar path, don't be afraid. Though uncertainty may cloud your vision, He sees beyond what you perceive—He knows the strength resting dormant within you, even when you don't. His wisdom surpasses all understanding, His plans are etched in eternity, perfectly designed for His glory. He knew that Wayne would complete me and I him—not as mere partners, but as two hearts, crafted by His hands, molded to strengthen each other's weaknesses, to stand united in a ministry that reflects His perfect love. Alone, we are fragments. Together, we fulfill the call that He breathed into existence.

It is time to cast aside our doubts, to let go of the reins we so tightly clutch, and to relinquish all control into His sovereign hands. Trust me when I say that life is richer, fuller, and more radiant when surrendered to His will. The ministry we walk in was never meant to be defined by human labels—it is not merely an individual mission or a Children's Ministry. No, it is His ministry, a divine outpouring of grace reaching into the depths, touching lives once forgotten, lifting the weary, restoring the broken, calling home the least of these.

I know what it is to be the least—to feel discarded, invisible, unworthy of love. I once bore the weight of loneliness, hopelessness, and brokenness so profound that it seemed inescapable. But God, in His mercy, saw beyond my sorrow. He reached into the darkness and pulled me into His marvelous light. He revealed the tapestry of His love, woven into every tear, every doubt, every silent cry. If you, too, wrestle with those same burdens, hear this truth: those whispers of inadequacy, of unworthiness—they are nothing more than lies spun by the enemy. You are not discarded. You are cherished. You are seen. You are deeply loved by the One who set the stars in place and breathed life into the universe. He has called you by name; and in His embrace, you will find not just healing—but purpose, belonging, and the immeasurable depth of His love.

That moment stirs another memory—one of divine appointment, where God led me to minister to a soul in desperate need. We were traversing the vast landscapes of Canada, holding children's services, revivals, and teacher trainings, sowing seeds of faith wherever we went. On one particular evening, the pastor extended an unexpected invitation: Would I preach to the adults in the congregation? I sensed immediately that God was moving in an extraordinary way—not directing His message to just one heart, but to many. As the service concluded, I wove through the crowd, my spirit attuned to those in need. Then, I saw her—a woman seated in the very last row, her head bowed so deeply, it was as if the weight of the world had anchored her to the seat, crushing her beneath burdens unseen—yet deeply felt. To my astonishment, no one was praying with her. As I drew closer, an undeniable stirring arose within me. God's voice was clear—He wanted to speak life into her weary soul. Yet the moment I spoke, I met a force unlike any I had encountered before. An invisible wall of resistance, thick and immovable, clung to her like a suffocating shroud. Each time I declared God's truth, a guttural growl escaped her lips—an open defiance, a battle against the very love that sought to rescue her. Still, I pressed on.

"God loves you," I assured her. "No, He doesn't," she spat back, her voice sharp with pain. "Yes, He does," I countered, unwavering. Over and over, the exchange continued, a war between darkness and light. The more I spoke, the more vehemently she rejected the words—but I refused to retreat. A righteous determination rose within me, a divine certainty that she *mattered.* This battle wasn't just about her—it was about every wound, every lie, every stronghold the enemy had shackled her with. A righteous anger sparked within me. This moment was a battlefield, and I refused to let the enemy claim her spirit. *Not today, devil, Not today!* I thought. *Not this one. She matters.* Sensing the need for greater spiritual fortitude, I turned to two nearby women and called them to join me in prayer. A united front was necessary—a force of faith to break through the chains gripping her soul. Slowly, almost imperceptibly at first, her head began to lift. As her head slowly lifted, it was more than just a physical movement—it was a silent rebellion against the forces that had tried to keep her down. Each inch upward was a defiance against despair, a quiet declaration that hope was stirring once more—and for the first time—our eyes met. What I saw shook me to the core. Her gaze held the weight of years—of battles fought in silence, of suffering too immense to voice. Pain was etched into every line of her face, exhaustion lingering in her very posture. She was *tired,* worn from the fight, teetering on the edge of surrender.

I softened, lowering my voice to a whisper, a promise carried in the quiet. "It's going to be okay." We talked for an hour or so—just the two of us, soul to soul. Then something

126

shifted. The resistance cracked, even if it was just slightly. The walls weren't impenetrable, they could fall. God would break through in a way only He could. Slowly, as if the heavens themselves had intervened, her burdens began to lift. The crushing pressures that had nearly broken her spirit eased, as the grace of God poured over her like a healing balm. I knew, at that moment, that she had been seen, known, and loved. God had orchestrated this encounter because He understood—her heart needed more than fleeting words; it needed time and personal attention. A reminder that His love was relentless. And as that truth settled within her, the transformation was undeniable.

That day, a bond was forged, a friendship that would endure. As we parted, I embraced her in a healing hug—a gesture I had once received when I, too, needed the warmth of human kindness. Over the following year, I watched God work in miraculous ways, restoring her relationships, rekindling her faith, breathing new life into her weary spirit. Her journey was far from over, but the woman who had once hidden beneath the weight of despair now walked in strength. She had learned to fight the good fight of faith, her heart now radiant with hope. Her transformation was evident—inside and out. And it all happened because someone refused to walk past her pain, then took the time to remind her... she was *never* alone. God was with her. Leading, guiding, loving—always.

God's healing is never just about restoration—it's about transformation. He mends our wounds so that we, in turn, might become vessels of hope and strength for others. There is a profound unique beauty in understanding, and nothing cultivates that more deeply than personal experience. When we ourselves have walked through the fire, we can offer not just empathy, but the kind of understanding that speaks directly to the soul.

But that raises the real question: Are we willing to step forward, to reach out from the depths of our own pain—the kind that once threatened to consume us? Vulnerability is a daring choice, yet it is in sharing our scars that we truly touch lives. Over time, I have found solace in the testimony of others. Watching someone rise from the ashes I once sat in gives my spirit fresh hope, reminding me that victory is not just possible, it's promised.

Likewise, I have deep admiration for those who have walked in unwavering truth from the beginning. Their steadfastness is a testament to the power of faith through time, standing as an anchor against the storms of life. In ministry, both perspectives are essential—the tested and the steadfast. Each carries a weight of wisdom the other cannot fully grasp alone. One of the greatest influences in my life was a soul nurtured in God's love, raised in a family that radiated His presence. That love—pure, unwavering, and relentless—changed me in ways I never imagined. It is a love I long to reflect, a light I pray my life will mirror in its fullness.

No matter the path we've taken—whether scarred by trials or steadfast from the start—our stories bear His fingerprints. God longs to enhance every page of our life. He longs to redeem our experiences and turn them into something far greater than we could conceive. His vision transcends ours, and when we fail to seek His perspective, we rob ourselves of His boundless purpose. So let us stand—whatever our testimony, whatever our journey—and allow Him to use it for His glory.

To the one who is struggling, I ask you—are you ready to step forward and embrace the healing prescription God has written just for you? It's been long enough. Aren't you weary— tired of hurting, of wrestling against the weight of your burdens, of hiding behind a smile that doesn't reflect your heart? I know that weight. I've worn that mask. And admitting you need help— real help—might be the hardest step. But I understand because I've stood exactly where you stand now. I've felt the suffocating grip of fear, the endless spiral of doubt, the heaviness of the struggle. But there comes a moment when you must choose—to trust that God sees you, knows you, and holds your life securely in His hands. Whether you have battled hardships your entire life or the battle emerged under the weight of ministry, He knows. He sees. He understands.

I never imagined I would be where I am today. I never felt worthy of doing anything for God. But I've learned—it isn't worthiness, it's about *willingness.* Willingness to heal. Willingness to surrender. Willingness to step into the unknown and let God use you for His purpose. After all, didn't God use a donkey to deliver His message? That story remains one of my favorite reminders that God can use anyone, at any moment, for

His divine will. It is a testament that in Him, we are all possibilities.

It is not about being perfect. I've stumbled, failed, and fallen—and I will again. Even David, the psalmist, the warrior, the king—made devastating mistakes. And yet he was still called a man after God's own heart. Why? Because David was willing to acknowledge his imperfection. He wasn't defined by his failures but by his relentless love for God and his willingness to cry out, to repent, and to seek restoration. And *that* is where it all begins—with true repentance, poured out from a heart that dares to be honest before God. It is okay to be raw with God, to admit your doubts, to confess your fears, to acknowledge your failures. The problem is never the mistakes themselves, it's allowing those mistakes to hold you hostage.

You deserve joy in Him. It is okay to smile again, to laugh—even when the storm still rages. Because here's truth: God is working, even in the unseen, even in the silence—and that confuses the enemy. *"Why are they smiling?"* he wonders. We smile because we have learned to trust that God is in control—not just when the skies are clear, but even in the storm. We smile because we know that beyond the dark clouds, sunshine awaits. Faith begins with sight—not with the physical eye, but with the eyes of your heart. And when you choose to see beyond the trial, joy will follow. Life will become beautiful again, because there is power in a merry heart. Go ahead—try it—smile. Jesus loves you. And never forget this: The joy of the Lord is your strength.

Eight: When Heaven Whispers

Because Some Opportunities Don't Knock Twice

*T*here are moments in life when we feel inadequate—convinced we're too flawed to be used by God. We believe perfection is a requirement, that only flawless lives are worthy of His calling. In the earlier years of my ministry, I struggled with these lies. I wrestled with doubt, often asking, *"Who am I?"* as if Jesus required qualifications instead of surrender.

One afternoon, my youngest daughter, Caylie, and I found ourselves in the prayer room of the church where we were ministering. The evenings were reserved for services, but the days were our sanctuary—our quiet time to rest and seek the presence of God. As we began to pray, something in the atmosphere shifted. The air thickened with His presence, and an undeniable force pressed upon my spirit, compelling me to my knees. Tears cascaded down my face as the voice of the Lord resonated within my soul, weaving scripture into the depths of my being:

"If my people, who are called by my name, will humble themselves and pray and seek my face and turn from their wicked ways, then I will hear from heaven, and I will forgive their sin and will heal their land." 2 Chronicles 7:14 NIV

At that moment, there was no mistaking it—the Lord was speaking directly to my heart. A wave of conviction washed over me as I realized what He was asking. I had to surrender—not just my doubts, not just my fears, but my very *self*. It was never about *who I was*, but about *who He is*. Jesus was calling me deeper, beckoning me into a walk of absolute trust, a journey of complete reliance on Him. That day, my heart went deeper, stripped of its pretense, stripped of its pride and humbled before the magnitude of His grace. I cried out, *"Yes, Lord."* I didn't have much to offer, but what I had, I gave. And if He could use someone like me—I was willing.

The presence of God was so tangible, so strong, that my daughter was swept up in it as well. As tears streamed down her face, I realized that she, too, was encountering Him in a way she never had before. I reached for her hand, and together, we knelt—mother and daughter—sobbing before the Lord as His

Spirit moved over us. That moment marked us. It changed something. He was preparing us for the road ahead.

I believe it still—now more than ever. The voice of God is calling His Church to awaken, to cast off the veil of slumber and return to Him in humility. There can be no hesitation, no compromise. He calls us to turn from our wicked ways—and yes, I said *wicked ways.* For sin is not only found in rebellion or corruption, but also in the quiet chambers of pride, the gnawing doubt that erodes faith, the creeping fear that silences boldness, and the weight of complacency that keeps His people stagnant.

Humility is painful; it strips us bare before the presence of a holy God. Yet, it is necessary. It is cleansing. It is the posture of surrender that leads to revival. We are the people of the Name— the Name above all names, the mighty Name of Jesus. He is speaking—not in distant echoes, but in the present, in the urgent now. He speaks to us, His Church, and the time to listen, to act, to return—is today.

If we truly live in truth, we must seek Him daily. Pray—not out of routine, but out of hunger. Listen—not passively, but with expectation. And cast off the lies that whisper, *God can't use me,* or *He doesn't desire to heal me.* For He *can,* and He *does.*

Looking back, we often understand our struggles more clearly—but do we truly grasp their purpose? Do we recognize the value of the battle? God doesn't use hardships to punish us; He uses them to refine us—to shape our hearts for His Kingdom. And if we surrender to that process, He will take what the enemy

133

meant for destruction and transform it into an instrument for His glory.

This truth became vividly clear one night at Junior Camp in Texas. The altars were packed with children—hands lifted, hearts desperate and hungry to experience the power of God. The atmosphere was charged with the power of the Holy Ghost as countless souls stepped into their breakthrough. But as I scanned the room, something unexpected happened—I nearly stumbled over a small child standing quietly behind me. Turning, I met the beaming face of J.J., a young boy who had received the Holy Ghost the previous night. His face was shining, his eyes lit with joy, and everything about him radiated confidence in the Spirit. I could feel him watching me closely, mimicking every word and action. I leaned in to hug him, but before I could, an adult grabbed my arm and hurried me away.

On the other side of the room, a small group had been praying tirelessly with another young boy—one who had been seeking the Holy Ghost night after night without a breakthrough. He was *desperate*, yet his prayers remained unanswered. Feeling defeated, someone in the group suggested that I pray with him. As I approached, the crowd instinctively stepped aside, their faces etched with fatigue and disappointment. I began to pray, but immediately sensed resistance—a barrier, a heaviness in the spirit. One of the adults turned to me and asked, *"What now?"* Without hesitation, I responded, *"We pray."* Prayer isn't merely words—it's *seeking*. And sometimes, when resistance stands tall, you stop praying *for* the individual and *seek the face of God.*

134

Within moments, I heard it—clear as a bell in my spirit. *"J.J!"* I turned, and there he was, standing behind me. The group had prayed fervently for over an hour. *Nothing.* No tears, no movement, no response, Heaven stood silent. I looked at J.J., and I just knew. Something in my spirit lit up.

"J.J.," I said, "I don't know what you're supposed to say, but Jesus wants you to speak to this young man."

Without fear, without hesitation, J.J. stepped forward. He gently placed his arm around the boy's head and whispered something in his ear. I don't know what he said to this day—but I know what happened next. Tears burst from the boy's eyes, his lips quivered, and suddenly, he began to speak in tongues— loudly, freely, beautifully. And in that moment, Jesus spoke again: *"Train up a child."*

At that moment, I understood what the Lord was saying. It was never about *what I could do*, but about *what He desired to do*. That day, He chose J.J. to lead a soul into His presence. That moment wasn't just about a breakthrough for one boy—it was about building J.J.'s faith, preparing him for a journey ahead that would require unshakable trust. Back home, J.J. had a brother who was facing a battle with cancer—a battle that would be victorious but difficult. God was preparing *not just one heart, but many.*

God is always speaking. The real question is: *Are we listening?* If we take the time to learn from our challenges, we'll see that God isn't only directing our steps—He's weaving divine

135

appointments into the fabric of our everyday lives. Moments that, if we're not careful, we'll rush past. And how often do we miss them? How many opportunities slip through our fingers because we're too distracted, too busy, too consumed by the demands of daily life?

Ministry often means long hours on the road—miles upon miles of travel, with just enough time for quick meals and even quicker gas stops. Truthfully, I rarely look forward to those interruptions. To me, they often feel like delays—unwelcome detours from what I perceive as the "real" purpose ahead. But one particular stop reminded me that God's purpose sometimes finds us exactly where we'd rather not be.

My husband, Wayne, and I were enroute to the next church when I woke to the truck slowing to a stop. *"We need gas,"* he said simply. I glanced around at our surroundings, and immediately, frustration took hold. *Why here?* The station was small, dingy, and clearly neglected. Cleaning was not a priority. Annoyed but left with no choice, I stepped inside, only to find the women's restroom shut down for construction. *"Now what?"* I grumbled. After searching around the store, I spotted a line of ladies snaking outside a repurposed men's restroom. *This day just keeps getting better,* I thought sarcastically as I took my place at the very back of the line. Forcing a polite smile at the woman in front of me, I received a warm *"Hello"* in return. That simple exchange opened the door to conversation, and soon, we were deeply engaged. As we spoke, the line in front of us grew shorter until finally, it was just the two of us standing alone.

Then, realization hit, no one had lined up behind me. And that's when I felt it—the unmistakable nudge of the Holy Spirit: *"This is an opportunity to minister."* Had I remained consumed by my own irritation, I would have missed it.

The young woman shared that she had recently moved to a new state and was working as a delivery driver. The long hours behind the wheel, combined with being in an unfamiliar place, had left her feeling isolated and spiritually dry. She felt disconnected from God, unsure of how to find her way back. As she spoke, tears welled in her eyes. She wasn't just making conversation—she was crying out for help. She needed *assurance*—a reminder that she had not been abandoned. And in that moment, I set my frustration aside and *listened.*

When she hugged me goodbye, it wasn't a casual embrace. It was a hug soaked in gratitude—a quiet thank you for being present, for seeing her, for reminding her that God hadn't forgotten her. And as I walked away, I couldn't help but wonder—how many moments like that have I missed? How often does God place divine encounters before us, only for them to go unnoticed because we fail to *pause and listen*?

That wasn't the first time I had almost missed a divine appointment. I'll be honest with you—this day was one of *those* days. The kind where everything goes wrong, patience is thin, and frustration clings to you like an unwanted shadow. We were struggling financially, raising four children who seemed to grow

137

faster than we could keep up. Every single day was an act of trusting God to provide.

That morning, I woke up to find a flat tire. Not surprising, really. Our van ran on used tires—what Wayne and I called "Maypops," because they may pop... or they may not. Either way, we had no money for new ones. Wayne gently asked if I could use my day off to look for a replacement. I agreed. How hard could it be? Famous last words.

The first shop took one look at the van and smirked. "We don't carry tires that old." The second shop wasn't any better—dismissive, cold, and quick to send me on my way. Still, I pressed on. Shop after shop, rejection after rejection. Until finally, I gave up. I slumped behind the steering wheel, forehead resting on my hands, and whispered, "What now, God?" My voice was hollow. Why had I wasted the entire day chasing a tire that didn't seem to exist? That's when the conviction settled in. Why hadn't I prayed before I started? That simple question hit hard, so I did. I prayed—not a long, poetic prayer. Just a desperate plea, and as soon as I said, "Amen," a thought dropped into my spirit. One last shop, a small, obscure place across town I hadn't visited in years. "Why not?"

With renewed faith, I entered the store. *"You probably don't have this size, but..."* The attendant barely let me finish. *"We do. How many do you need?"* Tears threatened to spill as I choked out, *"Just one today. But I'll need more soon."* He nodded, took my keys, and motioned me toward the waiting room. Something about the atmosphere felt... different. The normally bustling shop was empty. Silent. Moments later, the attendant returned—but not with bad news. *"Excuse me, ma'am?"* A flicker of unease stirred in me. *"Please don't tell me you don't have the tire."* *"Oh no, ma'am. We have plenty. But..."* He hesitated, his voice growing quieter. *"I need to talk to you."* Curious, I listened. He shared a story that shifted *everything*. The previous night, he and his young daughter had prayed together. She had felt a stirring in her heart—a call to return to church. He quickly agreed, but uncertainty emerged over which church they should attend. He knew not just any church would do, he desired a church that preached truth. "We prayed for God to send an angel to guide us," he said softly. *"And when you walked in, God said, "There is your angel."* This time, the tears didn't just threaten—they fell.

Had I prayed *at the beginning of my day,* God could have directed me straight to John and his daughter. How many souls go untouched simply because we fail to pray, *"Lead me, Lord"* before stepping out? That Sunday, John and his daughter joined me at church. Their faith was renewed, their journey back to God had begun.

After I drove home, I rested my head against the steering wheel once more—this time, not in frustration, but in awe. Humbled. Grateful. That day, I had two choices: to see it as an inconvenience or as an opportunity to be used by God. Every day is filled with divine appointments; the question isn't *if* they're there—it's *whether we're listening.* And listening requires more

139

than just hearing—it requires *intentional stillness.* Not just pausing our schedule but pausing our spirit. Tuning our hearts like an instrument until even the faintest whisper of heaven resonates deep within.

I'll be honest—there have been days when I missed Him entirely. Days when the noise of life was louder than my faith. Days when I tried to do everything in my own strength— problem-solving, overthinking, controlling—until I finally wore myself out. And only then would I fall to my knees and say, "Lord, what do You want me to do?" We live in a world that doesn't stop. The notifications don't stop. The demands don't stop. But God... He still speaks. And when we slow down— when we shut out the noise—we find that He's been there all along.

I sense someone reading this needs a deeper kind of encouragement. You know God uses you. You know He speaks through you. But right now... *you're the one in need.* I've been there.

During chemotherapy, I learned what it meant to cling to the smallest threads of hope. Every day was a battle. Pain so constant and suffocating that even walking across the room felt like scaling a mountain. The medication dulled everything—my energy, my thoughts, even my sense of self. Some days, all I could do was sit in silence and listen to the voices of my family, unable to answer, unable to reach back. I felt lost inside my own body.

Yet even as I fought through weakness, bills continued to pile up. One afternoon, I walked to the mailbox, clutching a faint hope that perhaps—*somehow*—relief had arrived. Instead, I found a stack of bills waiting for me, staring back like silent tormentors. One stood out—the mortgage. It was *due immediately.* I looked down at our checkbook, as though somehow, miraculously, it would contain the funds we lacked. That's when I broke. The tears came hard and fast. I dropped the bills on the counter and collapsed into a heap. That news felt like the final straw. Just then, Wayne walked in, instantly taking in my crumpled form and tear-streaked face. *"Baby, what's wrong?"* he asked, worry threading through his voice as he wrapped me in his arms. Between sobs, I whispered, *"It's the house payment. It's due, and we don't have the money."* He held me tighter, his words gentle but unwavering. *"Baby, God will supply. Don't worry yourself."* I wanted to believe him. Oh, how I *wanted* to. But fear still clung to my heart. And then—God stepped in.

The very next morning, as I stood in the kitchen cooking breakfast, we heard an unexpected knock. Wayne and I exchanged glances, startled by the interruption. *"Who would be here on a Saturday—at the back door?"* Wayne opened it, and just as he did, an envelope fluttered to the ground, landing softly at his feet. Confused, he bent down, picking it up. *"What do we have here?"* he murmured, curiosity laced with caution. He tore it open, and both of us froze. Inside was cash—enough to cover our mortgage in full. Emotion overwhelmed us. We ran outside, searching the yard, scanning the street. But no one was there. No car speeding away. No neighbor slipping back into their home. Just the wind... and God. To this day, we still don't know who left that envelope. Maybe it was an angel on assignment, or maybe it was a vessel whose obedience delivered our miracle. But we *do* know this—God provided. That envelope was more than a rescue. It was a reminder. A whisper from heaven that said, *I see you. I haven't forgotten you. I'm still here.* It was another brick in the foundation of our faith. Another moment in the slow, sacred process of learning to trust God—not just when it's easy, but when it feels impossible. He reminded us, once again, that He is faithful beyond understanding, beyond circumstance. That day was more than a financial rescue—it was another step in the journey of faith, another lesson in surrender, another moment in learning to *trust Him completely*. Even when doubt tries to creep in, even when all human solutions fail, even when you *don't see* the answer—God is already working.

Chemotherapy was an unrelenting storm, a force that swept through my life, leaving nothing untouched. Every day became a battle against pain so overwhelming that even the smallest movements felt like climbing a mountain. Tumors pressed against my body, making even the act of standing a distant dream. The agony forced me into reliance on morphine and other medications—heavy chains that shackled me to a world of lethargy and silence. I remember hearing my family's voices as they came home—concerned, gentle, trying to reach me. But I was trapped. I couldn't respond. I couldn't move. I couldn't lift my eyes. I was alive... but not really living. My days blurred into long stretches of medicated sleep. My mind grew clouded with

142

sadness and helplessness. The weight of it was unbearable. I couldn't understand why God allowed the suffering to continue, why He had left me in this hollow existence. Had I failed to trust Him? Had I done something to deserve this? Those questions became my constant companions as my situation spiraled downward. The doctor, seeing my decline, called in palliative care, and soon a nurse arrived each week to check my medications and monitor my wellbeing. Months passed in this haze until the nurse informed me that she'd be going on vacation. I was expected to call the main office for a replacement, but something inside me rebelled at the thought. I was exhausted—not just physically, but spiritually and emotionally. This wasn't living. I was just existing, locked in a prison of drugs and pain, disconnected from everything that made me feel human. I wanted out. I hated how the medication dulled my senses, how it stole every ounce of vitality I had left. The thought of continuing like this—trapped and muted—felt unbearable. I decided: when the nurse left, I would stop taking the medication. All of it. Cold turkey. I knew she'd warned against it, but I didn't care. My desperation drowned out her voice. I convinced myself, *"If God is truly God, He'll deliver me."*

I was naïve to the nightmare that awaited me. What followed was more than suffering—it was pure torment. The withdrawal gripped me in its unforgiving claws, shaking me to my very core. My body convulsed, trembling beyond control, refusing rest, refusing peace. One night, Wayne begged me to get up—his exhaustion weighed heavy, and he needed sleep for work the next morning. But I couldn't stop shaking. My mind screamed in confusion; my body rebelled against me. I was a prisoner of my own decisions.

I paced the halls, whispering over and over, "I am a child of God. I am a child of God." The words became my lifeline, my desperate plea for strength. The nausea was merciless, hitting in wave after wave. I found myself rushing to the bathroom again and again, overwhelmed by sickness and pain. "Lord, please make it stop!" I cried into the void, searching for relief. But none came. Was He listening? Was He watching me suffer, unmoved? Had I made a mistake by taking matters into my own hands? The nights became endless rotations of pacing and weeping, of aching prayers sent into silence. Sleep was a luxury I no longer had, and the agony felt like it would never end. And then—after days of torment—the storm began to lift. The shaking slowed. My thoughts cleared. I could finally breathe. It was in that fragile moment of clarity that I finally heard Him. I was praying, still trying to grasp the weight of what I had endured. "God, why?" The question was whispered through trembling lips, born of exhaustion, of desperate need for understanding. And then, His voice—a still, small presence, soft but undeniable. "Now you understand the addict."

The words shattered something in me. I collapsed into the chair, weeping uncontrollably. My spirit broke wide open under the weight of that simple, devastating truth. "Forgive me, Jesus," I sobbed. I hadn't just been battling physical pain—I had been battling pride, desperation, and the dangerous lie that I could

144

handle it on my own. I had ignored wisdom. I had bypassed prayer. I had traded trust for control. And in doing so, I had walked straight into a torment I didn't understand—until now. I had suffered, yes. But I wasn't the only one. And now... I finally understood the suffering of someone addicted, someone bound in a way they can't simply pray away. Someone trapped by something that once promised relief but turned into a prison. My pain had purpose. Not because I handled it perfectly—I didn't. But because God, in His mercy, used my mistake to teach me something sacred. I saw the addict differently now. I didn't pity them. I didn't judge them. I *understood* them.

Would I ever willingly endure such an ordeal again? Never. Would I advise anyone to go through withdrawal alone? Absolutely not. There are resources. There is help. No one should ever endure what I went through in silence. But I thank God... Because through it all, He gave me a burden I hadn't carried before.

Now, when I see someone bound by addiction, I don't just see the struggle—I feel it. I hear it. I know it. Because I've lived it. Even if just for a short time, I walked through that valley. And what the enemy meant for harm, God used to birth a deeper compassion inside me.

And I will never—never—forget it.

Opportunities to minister often arrive quietly, tucked into the corners of ordinary moments we least expect. Sometimes they require patience—a willingness to step back and let God

145

work in His perfect timing, trusting that He alone draws hearts to living waters.

During a revival in Oklahoma, I watched as a woman poured her heart into seeking the Holy Ghost, her desire evident in every longing glance toward the altar. For months, she had pursued this gift, yearning for the breakthrough that never seemed to come. Meanwhile, her husband—who had just started attending church with her—received the Holy Ghost almost immediately, as did the friends she had invited. One by one, they stepped into the promise, their lives visibly changed. But for her, it remained just out of reach.

She smiled through the joy of others, but I could see it: the quiet frustration creeping in like a slow fog. Night after night, when the altar call came, I hoped to stand beside her, to pray with her. But she always slipped out before I could reach her— retreating before the moment could unfold. My heart ached in ways words couldn't express. But I knew: this was not a door I could force open. It had to be God's timing.

So, I carried her in prayer, whispering her name into heaven from the quiet of my hotel room. But it didn't feel the same. A restlessness stirred within me. I couldn't understand why she hesitated—why something seemed to hold her back. That very night, God so graciously reminded me of my own struggle. A time when I had wrestled with the very same hesitation, the same feelings of not being worthy, not being ready. That memory softened me. "Okay, Lord," I whispered, "I'll wait."

One night remained. My hope burned bright—surely, knowing this was the final service, she would step forward. She just had to. Yet as the congregation slowly dispersed, I saw her again, moving swiftly toward the exit. Disappointment lodged itself deep in my heart, aching deep within. We packed our trailer in silence, the weight of unfulfilled longing pressing heavily on my mind. I fought back the sting of tears, knowing I couldn't force her breakthrough. I had done all I could. The rest was up to God.

Soon, the excitement of a long-awaited family reunion began to replace the sorrow. By morning, we would be on our way to Arkansas. My heart warmed at the thought of embracing my mother and sister again—it had been nearly a year since I had last seen them. Thoughts of laughter, shared stories, and the familiarity of home filled my mind, pulling me toward joy. Fun-filled days stretched ahead, and I allowed myself to sink into anticipation, to savor the coming moments.

Then the phone rang. The sound yanked me from my thoughts, jolting me back to reality. I picked it up, unsure of what to expect. It was the pastor from the church we had just left. His voice carried urgency, but also something else—excitement. He apologized for the late call, but his next words chased away all weariness. "She wants to meet with you," he said. My breath caught. The woman who had slipped away every night—the one whose breakthrough I had prayed for in silence—wanted to meet us. Privately. One-on-one. "She asked if you would be willing to meet her at the hotel tomorrow morning." he said, and the spark inside me ignited into a flame. "Of course," I said without hesitation. The pastor paused. "Are you sure? I know you've been looking forward to seeing your family. I don't want to keep you from that." But there was no conflict in my spirit. I knew immediately. "Yes," I told him. "We're sure." I meant every word. I wanted to see my family—I truly did—but this? This was more important. This was the very thing we had been praying for. And I knew—my family would understand. This was ministry. This was purpose. This was God's perfect timing.

Morning couldn't come fast enough. I barely slept—caught between anticipation and the lingering doubt that she might back out again. What if fear overtakes? What if the enemy whispered one more lie into her ear and she slipped away, like she had so many nights before? But right on schedule, she arrived, her pastor by her side, stepping into the space where God had drawn us together.

We agreed on the breakfast room, neutral and unassuming, a place where conversation could unfold naturally. As Wayne busied himself loading the truck, I sat down with her, feeling the nervous energy radiating from across the table. She was on the brink of running. I could feel it. Not today. No way, enemy. This stops here.

Softly, I greeted her, my voice calm, steady, though my spirit surged with urgency. I asked how she felt, though I already knew—she was unraveling, a tangled mess of nerves and self-doubt. Then, the apology spilled out, fragile and hesitant. She admitted she had no explanation for why she ran each night of the revival. She just did. Shame flickered in her eyes, a war she had carried far too long. I let out a small, reassuring laugh. "It's alright," I told her. "You're here now. That was what mattered." We talked—long and deeply, peeling back layers she had never dared to share before. She spoke of her fears, her frustrations, the battle raging inside her. It was more than hesitation. It was decades of baggage—wounds unseen, whispered lies of unworthiness, chains she had never known how to break. Each confession was a weight released, and with each word, the conversation began to turn.

As she poured out her heart, I began to feel a shift in the atmosphere. Slowly, almost imperceptibly, the breakfast room started to empty. Guests who had been eating just moments before filtered out one by one, as if guided by an unseen hand. It wasn't loud. We weren't causing a scene. But something Holy was happening. Then, the most unexpected thing occurred. Without being asked, the breakfast attendant walked over and closed the doors leading into the main hotel. I froze. I recognized what was happening. This wasn't a coincidence—this was God clearing the room. Breakfast hours weren't over, yet here we were, alone.

She looked around, startled. "I'm sorry," she whispered again, her voice shaking. "I should've gone to the altar when I had the chance…" She had carried this regret, letting it weigh her down, letting it tell her lies. I leaned in, my voice gentle but

149

firm. *"What's wrong with here?"* I asked. *"You don't have to be in church to receive the Holy Ghost. Look around—God has already prepared the space."* Cautiously, she glanced around and saw it. The empty room. The quiet. The presence lingering in the air. I reached across the table and took her trembling hands. *"The Spirit is already moving on you,"* I said. *"Yield to Him. Let Him speak."* At that moment Wayne entered, his work finished. Perfect timing. I gave him a quiet nod, and he joined us in prayer. The Holy Ghost stirred. Then—it happened. A tremble in her shoulders. A quiver in her lips. And suddenly, the floodgates opened. She broke through in tongues, the Spirit rushing through her like a mighty wind. Tears streamed down her cheeks as realization hit her, as joy burst forth in waves. *"I got it!"* she said, overwhelmed with emotion. I beamed, my heart soaring. *"You sure did. Now let the Lord use you. Do something great with this gift."* She nodded, her spirit blazing with new purpose. And then—she hugged us all. Her joy was unstoppable, pouring from her like light, illuminating everything around her. God had done it. In His way. In His timing. Not within the walls of a church, but right here—in a breakfast room, behind closed doors, in a moment only He could orchestrate.

Even the breakfast attendant, silently watching, felt it. She had questions—deep ones—because she had felt something she had never experienced before. If we are willing, God will move anywhere... even in the hotel breakfast area.

When we returned the next year, I saw it—the radiance on her face, the joy in her steps, the transformation written in her very posture. She wasn't the same woman who had once slipped out the back doors in fear. She was alive with purpose now, rooted in the confidence of who she had become in Christ. She prayed with others, arms stretched in faith, her voice steady, full of authority and grace. Each visit revealed more growth—more fire, more passion. Her hunger for God had only deepened, and it was evident in everything she did. She wasn't just attending church—she was the church.

It was the kind of moment that makes every sacrifice, every long drive, every tear-soaked altar worth it. Yet another name written down in glory—an opportunity almost lost. But God had already decided. She was His. And now—she knew it too.

Nine: Not Going Back

The Question That Changed Everything

T here are moments in life when time seems to pause, when the atmosphere shifts, and the presence of God becomes undeniable. The night He healed me felt like heaven itself opened and poured restoration straight into my weary soul. In that instant, the weight of every battle, every tear, and every unanswered question lifted. I thought my journey had reached its end—but I would soon discover it was only the beginning.

Back then, still new in my walk with God, I was grasping for understanding—uncertain of His divine blueprint for my life.

While studying the Word, I was drawn to John chapter 5, to the scene of the lame man at the pool of Bethesda, a man who had endured suffering for thirty-eight long years. Then, the unexpected happened—Jesus approached him and asked: *"Wilt thou be made whole?"* I paused. The question struck me as strange. Surely, the answer was obvious. Anyone trapped in a life of sickness and despair would desperately long for healing— wouldn't they? Why would Jesus even ask? But as I lingered in that verse, the weight of His words settled deep in my spirit. This wasn't a casual question. It wasn't just an offer to relieve suffering. Jesus wasn't merely offering a cure—He was extending an invitation to transformation. Healing wasn't the destination. It was the threshold to something greater. A turning point. A call to rise up and walk into a completely different life.

If you've received healing but still feel a stirring for more, you're not imagining things. You are right! Healing is only the beginning. *And once again, Jesus is inviting you to more than healing—to wholeness.*

When Jesus asks, *"Wilt thou be made whole?"* He's not just asking if we want relief from suffering. He's digging deeper— challenging us with a far more difficult question: *Suppose I heal you—are you ready to live differently? Are you prepared to walk away from the things that broke you?*

This question echoes in the heart of every person who's felt God's healing touch yet still wrestles with the grip of their past. You've experienced His presence. You've received moments of breakthrough. But somewhere in the depths of your soul, *you still hear the echoes of old wounds.* The enemy whispers reminders of the past, guilt resurfaces, doubt returns, torment and

154

shame cling to the edges of your mind. And yet—Jesus speaks again. He's calling you forward, not just to be touched but to be changed.

> *"Later Jesus found him at the temple and said to him, "See, you are well again. Stop sinning or something worse may happen to you." John 5:14 NIV*

Healing was never meant to be temporary. Jesus doesn't restore you so you can return to what wounded you. His healing is a doorway—an invitation to step into something deeper. A new life, a new identity, a higher purpose.

Sin is often defined as rebellion, but it's much more. It's the very thing that keeps us fragmented, divided, and distant from our true identity in Christ. To live in bitterness, to hold onto doubt, to carry unforgiveness, to be consumed by fear—these are chains that divide us from wholeness. They don't just affect our spirit—they create internal war: Mind against heart—Heart against will—Body against spirit.

For the longest time, I thought healing meant I'd be free from all the pain. That it would vanish. But the truth? God made me whole *in* the pain. He didn't wait for the storm to pass—He walked it with me.

Pain had become my identity. My fortress. I built walls around my heart so high that not even love could climb them. Trust was impossible. I didn't know how to live without the hurt. Letting it go felt like losing part of myself. Years later, during a quiet moment of reflection, I felt Jesus whisper those same words again: "Wilt thou be made whole?" But this time, I understood what He was truly asking...

"Are you willing to release the anger? The doubt? The bitterness? Do you trust Me to use your pain for My glory?"

I wish I had surrendered sooner. Years were wasted—years fighting battles that I didn't have to face alone. Years that could have been filled with joy instead of struggle. The truth was that I wasn't ready to let go. I clung to my pain as if it were my lifeline, when all along, Jesus was offering me something greater.

Healing is a gift, but *wholeness is a journey*—and many of us fight the very hands extended to help us. There were days when I resisted every person who tried to reach. Pastors, friends, brothers, sisters—people who sincerely loved me were met with walls of distrust. I made their efforts harder, not out of malice, but out of fear. The enemy whispered lies: *"They don't truly care." "How can they love someone like you?"* I believed the deception. I believed that trust was dangerous, that love was conditional, that people would always disappoint. But the truth is, there are souls who reach because they see beyond your pain—they see YOU. Not the version buried under pain—but the person God created.

Not everyone who pushes people away is bitter. Some are just scared. Some have been hurt so deeply that vulnerability feels like standing on a battlefield unarmed. But resisting healing

156

doesn't protect you—it prolongs the pain. Healing doesn't mean losing the church. It means *becoming* the church. Wholeness doesn't make you perfect—it makes you usable. It moves you from the one needing restoration to the one *offering* it. And the hardest truth I had to accept? It's not about me. It's not about you. It's about Jesus.

Wholeness is completion. It's the state in which nothing is missing, absent, or broken in your mind, body, or spirit. It's not just about being patched up—it's about being made new:
Entire—Restored—Secure.
To be whole is to move from:
Victim to Victor
Defeated to Conqueror
Broken to New in Him

Wholeness doesn't promise a life without hardship. It doesn't mean pain will never return or struggles will magically disappear. But it *does* mean those struggles will no longer control you. It means the pain won't define you. It means your identity is no longer rooted in what happened *to* you, but in what Jesus has done *for* you. You are a child of the King. You are loved beyond measure. You are called, chosen, and restored.

So, stop listening to the voices that say you're worthless. Stop letting your past dictate your future. You belong in the Kingdom of God. You are needed; you are vital. And still, Jesus is asking: *"Wilt thou be made whole?"*

Wholeness does not begin with comfort—it begins with confrontation. The mirror of truth is often the hardest to face. Before I could step into healing, I had to acknowledge the raw, unfiltered reality of who I had become. I was broken—a mess of anger, hardness, and self-preservation. My wounds had shaped me into someone who knew how to survive... but not how to live. Pain had taught me to build walls, to be guarded, to view love as a foreign language. But that was never the life Jesus had authored for me. At some point, I had to surrender. I had to believe that His wisdom was greater than my own, that His plan was not meant to hurt me but to heal me. Healing is not passive—it is an act of surrender, an intentional stepping into trust. But trust is often met with resistance. The mind becomes a battlefield, and the enemy wastes no time invading the territory of our thoughts. Doubt whispers through the cracks:

"Are you sure God cleansed you?"

"Are you even worthy?"

If I wasn't careful, I could have spiraled right back into the very bondage Jesus had already called me out of. The adversary thrives on hesitation—on moments where uncertainty lingers, when the truth wavers just enough for him to sneak in. But the Word of God silences him:

"But he was pierced for our transgressions, he was crushed for our iniquities; the punishment that brought us peace was on him, and by his wounds we are healed"—Isaiah 53:5 NIV

Jesus didn't endure the cross for partial healing—He bore the weight of agony so that we could be completely restored.

The blood of the Lamb is not symbolic—it is sovereign. It's powerful, all-consuming, undeniable. The crimson river that flowed from His side was no ordinary sacrifice; it was the price of wholeness, paid in full. Every wound He bore, every painful stripe upon His back, every drop of blood that fell—it carried your name. His body was bruised beneath the weight of our transgressions, crushed by sorrow that was not His own. With each piercing thorn, each agonizing breath, He endured what we could not, so that we might be free. Love wrapped in suffering, mercy intertwined with pain—He gave everything, so that grace would never be out of reach. Yet, when we entertain the enemy's whispers—when we hesitate to believe, when we question whether we deserve healing—*we unknowingly devalue that precious sacrifice.*

Imagine standing at the foot of the cross, gazing upon the Lamb of God as He breathes His final breath. His body torn and beaten, His love bleeding out for the sake of all mankind. Now, imagine looking into His eyes and telling Him, "Your sacrifice wasn't enough."

That is what we declare—perhaps not aloud, but with our actions—when we refuse to walk in the healing He has already provided. Every time we cling to pain instead of His promise, we reject what He died to give.

Healing is a divine exchange. It is not just about restoration; it is about responsibility. Once Jesus makes you whole, you must guard that healing. To return to what He rescued you from is to say that Calvary was optional. That the blood wasn't necessary. That the price was too high for a life you're not willing to live free.

How often do we unknowingly walk back into the prison He unlocked for us? How often do we hesitate at the threshold of freedom, lingering in the familiar shadows of past wounds? The truth is that healing requires movement. Faith demands forward motion. Wholeness is not a resting place—it is a calling. There comes a moment in every believer's life when the Lord asks: *"Wilt thou be made whole?"* This is no mere question. It is a reckoning—a divine crossroads. The choice is yours. Will you hesitate? Or will you step forward and claim the fullness of what He suffered to give you?

Wholeness is not for the faint of heart. It is for the brave. The ones who are done surviving and ready to start living. The ones who will not cheapen Calvary with hesitation. The ones who will not mock His sacrifice by settling for less than freedom. Step into it, own it, live it; the blood has already spoken.

There is an unspoken war that rages within those who have tasted brokenness—the relentless struggle between resistance and surrender. I have fought that battle. I've stood defiant in the face of pain, refusing to bow beneath its weight. As a child, I equated brokenness with weakness. My stepfather—unyielding and determined—sought to break me from my stubbornness. His belt was his weapon; his words were his command: *"Cry!"* he demanded. The sting of leather tore into my skin, but I clenched my jaw, steadied my breath, and *refused*. In my mind, if I broke, I would lose. If I cried, I was weak. Yet, I have learned that true strength is not found in resistance—it is found in surrender. The world teaches us that brokenness is shameful, that to crack beneath pressure is to fail. But Scripture whispers a different truth:

"But he said to me, 'My grace is sufficient for you, for my power is made perfect in weakness.'"

Therefore, I will boast all the more gladly about my weaknesses, so that Christ's power may rest on me. That is why, for Christ's sake, I delight in weaknesses, in insults, in hardships, in persecutions, in difficulties. For when I am weak, then I am strong.—2 Corinthians 12:9-10 NIV

True power is not found in defiance—it comes from being vulnerability, in the willingness to be shaped by the hands of the Master. For years, I mistook hardness for strength. I built walls so high that nothing, not love, not grace, not even healing—could reach me. But hardness isn't safety—it's a prison. It locks us inside the very pain that Jesus has already declared healed.

How many of us are doing the same? We brace ourselves, we build defenses, we keep others at arm's length—all the while crying out for connection, for hope, for change. And all the while, Jesus is whispering: *Let Me work. Trust Me.*

161

Healing isn't passive—it's an act of bravery. It's the willingness to be reshaped, remade, rebuilt. When a potter crafts a masterpiece, there are moments when the clay must be pressed, kneaded, and even broken to take its final form. Just like the clay must yield to the hands of the potter, so must we yield to the hands of God—not because we're being discarded, but because we're being reformed into something more beautiful than before.

What if brokenness isn't the end, but the beginning? What if weakness isn't failure, but an open door for God's strength to shine? Healing doesn't erase the past—it redefines it. It turns wounds into wisdom, pain into purpose, and brokenness into beauty. If you've spent years resisting—afraid to break, afraid to feel, afraid to trust—know this: Jesus doesn't break His people to discard them. He breaks them to rebuild them. Let go and trust the hands that formed you. Step into the wholeness He has prepared for you.

We often see our lives like a shattered mirror—its fractured shards catching slivers of light yet reflecting only distortion. We stare at the broken pieces, whispering inward, *"Look at this wreckage... What remains of me?"* Our hearts cry out to God, *"I don't want to be broken."* We wrestle with vulnerability, convinced strength means holding it all together, maintaining composure even as the weight of life presses down. Yet, true strength is found in surrender, in the letting go, in the sacred unraveling where Jesus begins His work. To truly walk with Him, we must be willing to bend... or even break. Our flesh—our thoughts, attitudes, self-made identities, and tightly held

162

perceptions—must be laid down at His feet. Brokenness isn't final, it's transformational.

The world tells us to patch the cracks, to conceal the imperfections, to wear strength like armor. But God sees the beauty in the breaking. He doesn't discard the shattered people— He gathers them, shapes them, and crafts something more radiant than before. We were never created to reflect ourselves; we were made to reflect Him. But when self or fear takes center stage highlighting pride, His light is obscured. It's time to let the cracks show—because it's through the broken places that His glory shines brightest.

It's not easy to break. It hurts—it stretches—it refines. But in the breaking, something sacred happens—we step forward into our purpose. *Mary's alabaster box cradled a treasure, a fragrance so rare, so costly—yet its beauty remained hidden, locked within the unbroken vessel. Only in surrender, in the breaking, did the perfume spill forth, filling the air with an aroma that spoke of love, of sacrifice, of worship. The shattered pieces bore witness to a devotion that could not be contained, an offering poured out without hesitation, without regret.*

In the same way, the anointing in our lives can't flow until we allow God to break through our outer shell. The pain we avoid may be the very process that releases His glory, the very surrender that unlocks the purpose. Only when we are broken can the fragrance of His presence spill out—filling every corner of our lives with evidence of His goodness. So, don't fear the breaking. Embrace it. For in it, His masterpiece is revealed.

Once again, the Master asks, "Are you ready to be made whole?" Are you ready to surrender—to lay down the weight of your wounds, the burden of your battles, the echoes of your past? Are you ready to hand every shattered piece to the One who already knows how to make them beautiful?

Trusting God does not guarantee a life without hardship. It doesn't promise clarity at every turn. Trust simply means you are willing to take a step—to try, to believe, even when the path ahead is hidden in shadow.

Looking back, I see shadows—traces of regrets, unmet longings, and choices I'd give anything to rewrite. The past is a relentless storyteller, whispering every misstep and lost opportunity like a story that refuses to end. I was blind—not physically—but grief and pain clouded my vision. I longed to be seen, to feel connected, to be loved in a way that didn't come with conditions or cost.

Just as the lame man at the pool of Bethesda had no concept of the miracle being offered to him that day, neither did I. For thirty-eight years, the man had known only struggle. It was his existence—the lens through which he viewed the world. I, too, lived in that place—grappling, surviving, unaware that something greater waited for me. I didn't recognize that the love the world gave—conditional, fleeting, wrapped in manipulation—was counterfeit. God Himself is love—pure, unchanging, eternal.

In truth, I feared love. I longed for it, but I couldn't bring myself to trust it. I was caught in the war between yearning and self-protection—craving kindness, yet terrified it would betray me. My spirit cried out, *"Is anyone there?"*

And God answered. He sent people—divine interruptions wrapped in human form. But I couldn't reach out. Shame held me hostage. I let my past write the script of my future. I let fear build walls around what God had sent to heal. And those people, those God-appointed moments—they walked away. I didn't blame them. But the ache of regret lingers, a shadow that stretches across time. I grieve not only the loss, but the weight of what could have been—those moments left unlived, those connections left unspoken. Opportunities once within reach, slipped through my fingers like sand, their absence forming gaps in the tapestry of my life. What might have been? I'll never know. Fear, that silent thief crept in and stole the gifts heaven had placed before me. And now, I sit with the echoes of what was meant to be, longing for the fragrance of blessings I once turned away. But perhaps not all is lost. Perhaps even in grief, there remains grace—a whisper that calls me forward, urging me to embrace the moments yet to come.

Friend, hear me. Feel the weight of these words, let them settle deep within your soul: Jesus doesn't merely offer healing—He offers wholeness. A restoration so complete that every fractured piece is placed back with precision, every wound is mended with grace. This is not just a repair; it is a rebirth. It is stepping into a life remade, sculpted by the hands of the Master, shaped with divine intention.

He doesn't simply fix what is broken—He creates anew. He calls you forward, past the remnants of what was, into the fullness of what can be. This is redemption in its purest form, love poured out without condition, mercy that reshapes the very essence of your being.

In Luke 8:43-44, we witness how personal God is: "And a woman having an issue of blood twelve years, which had spent all her living upon physicians, neither could be healed of any, came behind him, and touched the border of his garment: and immediately her issue of blood was stanched."

Focus on that word—*stanched.* In one divine moment, her affliction was halted. At the mere touch of Jesus, the chaos obeyed.

The passage continues: "And Jesus said, 'Who touched me?' When all denied, Peter and they that were with him said, 'Master, the multitude throng thee and press thee, and sayest thou, who touched me?' And Jesus said, 'Somebody hath touched me: for I perceive that virtue is gone out of me.' And when the woman saw that she was not hid, she came trembling, and falling down before him, she declared unto him before all the people for what cause she had touched him, and how she was healed immediately. And he said unto her, 'Daughter, be of good comfort: thy faith hath made thee whole: go in peace.'"

Two words leap off the page: *virtue* and *faith*.

The Greek word for *virtue* here is *dunamis*—miraculous power, divine strength, heaven's force. Jesus *felt* power leave Him. That moment was different. Crowds pressed in from every side. Dozens touched Him, brushed against Him. But only one touch pulled the miraculous into motion. Why? It wasn't about the crowd. It wasn't even about proximity. It was about faith. A thousand hands may reach for Him, but it's faith that unlocks His power. That day, the woman wasn't just healed—she was *made whole*. Restored. Redeemed. Seen.

And that same wholeness is within reach today. But first— you must touch Him with faith.

Do not settle for mere healing when Jesus is inviting you into something deeper. Wholeness is the true calling. Your struggle hasn't been in vain—it's the soil from which your testimony is meant to grow.

I never imagined I'd be walking the paths I now walk with Jesus. For so long, all I could see were my flaws, my failures. I would look in the mirror and ask, *Me? "Who am I, Lord?"* But God is not limited by our perception. He doesn't define us by our past—He defines us by His purpose. He sees past the veil we place over our own worth. Where we hesitate, He advances. Where we shrink back, He calls us forward. Where we see unworthiness, He sees redemption. We judge ourselves by our wounds—but He sees us through the lens of His blood. The only way forward is trust—wholehearted, unwavering surrender.

167

That's where wholeness begins. Not with perfection, not with performance—but with surrender. The moment you lay your fear, your shame, your brokenness at His feet, something shifts.

Right now—this moment—Jesus sees you. He's been waiting patiently, watching with love in His eyes, asking once again:

"Wilt thou be made whole?"

This is not a rhetorical question. It's a divine invitation; your answer carries weight. It is a vow, a turning point, a declaration that you will not live shackled to the ruins of your past.

Jesus is offering you something eternal. Something sacred. A life not defined by wounds—but by worship. Not limited by shame—but released in grace. A life where your pain becomes your platform and your story becomes someone else's lifeline. So, reach and step forward.

You, beloved, are a radiant soul in God's Garden. Perhaps life has pruned you—cut away things that once felt essential. But don't despair. The pruning is preparation. The Gardener is not careless. He knows exactly what needs to be removed so that you can thrive. Soon, His beauty in you will bloom.

Jesus, the Master Gardener, lovingly tends to the hearts of His people. With gentle precision, He cultivates growth— trimming back what hinders, nurturing what remains. He removes the burdens that choke your joy, waters the dry places, and strengthens your roots in Him. He longs for you to flourish—not just survive. He wants you to reflect His radiance, to bloom in holiness, to bear the fruits of His Spirit: love, joy, peace, long-suffering, gentleness, goodness, faith, meekness, temperance.

As you are made whole in Him, you are transformed—not by your own efforts, but by the work of His hands. His love is the sun that warms you. His Word is the rain that nourishes you. His Spirit is the wind that stirs your branches. And His grace is the soil that holds you steady.

You are no longer defined by what was cut away.

You are defined by what remains.

You are a living testimony—of His healing, of His faithfulness, of His unfailing love.

So, bloom, child of God.

Not in spite of the pruning—but because of it.

Ten: The Gift Within the Fracture

The Brilliance Only Brokenness Reveals

I held my breath as I raced toward the kitchen, my heart pounding like a drum in my chest. Moments earlier, the sharp crack of breaking glass followed by a startled gasp had jolted me upright. The fear that curled in my stomach told me that whatever had happened wasn't going to be good—especially since my youngest daughter, Caylie, was in there alone. As I rounded the corner, the scene unfolded like a slow-motion reel. Shattered glass glistened across the floor like fallen stars, tiny shards reflecting the overhead light in fractured brilliance. In the middle of it all stood Caylie, her small hands trembling as she cradled the broken remnants of a cherished piece. Tears streamed down her cheeks, their steady stream carving delicate tracks along her flushed skin. "It was an accident," she whispered, her voice barely audible through the lump in her throat. "I didn't mean to break it."

She had been reaching for an ingredient, lost in the simple joy of making pancakes, when she decided to pull herself up using the vent hood. It hadn't held her weight. In an instant, she—and everything balanced precariously on the stove tumbled down in a chaotic crash. Among the casualties lay the fat chef spoon holder—once part of my favorite collection, now reduced to irretrievable fragments. "I can fix it," she pleaded, desperation lighting her tear-filled eyes. I knelt beside her, reaching for her trembling hands, pressing them gently within my own. "It's okay, baby," I murmured. But she shook her head fiercely, her sobs punctuated by the same aching insistence: "I didn't mean to break it." I drew her into my arms, her trembling frame folding into mine. "Sweetheart," I soothed, "what matters is that you're not hurt. The spoon holder can be replaced—but you can't."

As we gathered the broken pieces, the weight of the moment settled over me like a revelation. How many times have I found myself holding the shattered fragments of my own life? How many times had I desperately clutched at broken dreams, broken relationships, broken faith—believing that if I just tried hard enough, I could fix what was broken?

There were seasons when the pain felt insurmountable, where my heart bore wounds so deep, they felt unhealable. I had been a prisoner of my own unhappiness, suffocating beneath the weight of circumstances I couldn't control. And yet, standing there with my daughter, watching her wrestle with her own sense of loss, I saw myself reflected in her despair. I wanted her to understand that accidents happen, that material things, no matter how sentimental, would always be fleeting. But my words felt like whispers against the storm of her sorrow. The image of her standing there, clutching broken pieces, her face streaked with tears, is one I will never forget.

And I wonder—does God see us in the same way? Fragile. Fractured. Holding shattered remnants, unsure how to move forward?

No one welcomes the pain of brokenness. It requires surrender. It requires letting go. It rarely makes sense in the moment. But if we would trust God, what seems like destruction can lead to revelation.

Would it shock us to learn that sometimes God *allows* brokenness? Not to harm us, but to refine us. Just as a parent says "no" to protect a child or teach them an invaluable lesson, God, in His infinite wisdom, knows that some things must be stripped away for us to be transformed. Piece by piece, He chisels away the rough edges of our lives—the bitterness, pride, and stubbornness. He knows that the weight of unforgiveness stunts growth. He understands that self-reliance, when wielded as an idol, blinds us from true dependence on Him.

Jesus spoke of this refining process:

"Very truly I tell you, unless a kernel of wheat falls to the ground and dies, it remains only a single seed. But if it dies, it produces many seeds. Anyone who loves their life will lose it, while anyone who hates their life in this world will keep it for eternal life."—John 12:24-25 NIV

A seed, untouched and unbroken, may carry the promise of life, yet it remains locked in solitude—unchanged, unfulfilled. But when it surrenders itself to the soil, when it falls, is buried, and dies, it's not lost—it's transformed. That death is not an end, but a beginning. Hidden beneath the earth, unseen by human eyes, something miraculous takes place: the husk breaks, the roots extend, and new life unfurls.

Is this not the very rhythm of redemption? Consider Christ—the seed of Heaven—who willingly embraced death, was laid in the tomb, and then rose in glory. Through His sacrifice, life was multiplied, and the barren places of the soul burst into bloom. In His surrender, He bore a harvest that continues to nourish hearts across generations.

And so, it is with us. To cling to our own will and, our own strength, is to remain unchanged, stagnant, alone. But to yield—to die to ourselves, to lay down our brokenness in trust—this is where true life begins. In the hands of God, what was once a single seed becomes a flourishing field, a rich and abundant harvest. God whispers, "You were never meant to remain buried. You were meant to rise."

When loss becomes our focus, we unknowingly limit ourselves to the remnants, holding onto what once was rather than embracing what could be. We grasp at fragments, our hands filled with broken pieces that can never restore what was whole—forgetting that restoration was never about returning to the past but stepping into something new, something greater.

That day, my daughter's eyes saw only the shattered spoon holder, a symbol of loss in her small world. What she didn't yet understand was the deeper truth waiting beneath the brokenness—the lesson wrapped in love, in grace, in perspective. Our bond, mother and daughter, was far richer than any object, more valuable than any possession. She was my treasure, my gift, my constant. No matter what life shattered, no matter how many storms came, she would always be my child.

That is the heart of a mother I want to be to all my children—a love unshaken by the weight of shattered things, a love that refuses to define her children by the cracks they carry. It is a love that sees past the brokenness, past the struggles and missteps, and instead beholds the masterpiece unfolding beneath it all. A mother does not merely see fragments—she sees possibility. She sees the promise of redemption, of growth, of beauty rising from places that once seemed beyond repair.

Her love does not falter when the storms come. It does not retreat when the world says something is too far gone. No, she presses in, believing that within every wound, within every failure, there is something sacred—something God Himself is shaping for a greater purpose. She holds her children not as broken vessels, but as radiant reflections of grace. And with unwavering devotion, she whispers to them what God whispers to us all: "You are not defined by what was lost. You are shaped by what is yet to be redeemed."

And isn't that the heart of God? No matter how fractured we feel, no matter how much we grieve over what seems beyond repair, He still calls us His own. He never sees us as merely broken. He sees the masterpiece He is forming through the cracks, the beauty He is bringing forth from the ashes.

When I look back on that moment, I don't see the shards scattered across the floor. I see the revelation. Because brokenness is never the final chapter—it is the beginning of God's most profound work, shaping us into something far greater than we ever imagined.

Although the test itself was grueling, nothing compared to the heartbreak of watching a loved one endure it. I have witnessed the weight of brokenness in all four of my children— their struggles etched deeply into my soul. I have seen my sons' tears trace silent paths down their faces, heard the anguished cries of my daughters, and felt their unspoken sorrow in the quiet moments between words. Each heartache, each desperate question, each whispered plea for understanding—I have carried them all in prayer.

Yet, through it all, I knew that they had been raised in strength and faith, and that, no matter how fierce the storm, this too would pass. Their childhood was never paved with ease. Not only did they shoulder the weight of our trials, but they bore their own burdens with quiet resilience and still do today.

Our youngest son endured relentless health battles—his early years woven with hospital rooms, unanswered questions, and nights filled with prayers. Yet, though his body bore the weight of struggle, his spirit remained unshaken. Those trials did not define him—they refined him, sculpting him into the extraordinary man he is today: Compassionate, kind, and unwavering. His journey was never easy, but it shaped him in ways that transcend the limitations once placed upon him. He has intimately known adversity, yet he continues to rise, proving with every step that challenge is not a life sentence, but a steppingstone to greatness. The labels that once clung to him have long since fallen away, unable to contain the depth of his strength and resilience. He is not his past struggles; he triumphs over them. His heart carries a wisdom beyond his years, a quiet strength that turns suffering into something beautiful—a strength I hear in the gentle sincerity of his voice every time he whispers, "I love you." Though life remains unkind, I hope he knows this truth beyond all doubt: He is deeply loved and cherished by his dad and me. He is a gift beyond measure, a testament to perseverance, a soul shaped not by what he has endured, but by how he continues to overcome.

Our older son bears the weight of severe ADHD and anxiety—a burden that presses heavily against his compassionate heart, amplifying every worry, every fear. He feels deeply, loves fiercely, cares endlessly, and at times, the sheer intensity of it all threatens to consume him. Yet, even during his struggles, his spirit remains unyielding, and his challenges only serve to deepen his passion for life. His heart is one of extraordinary kindness—a reservoir of encouragement, wisdom, and quiet strength. His purpose is woven into the way he teaches, inspires, and uplifts those who cross his path. He may not see it, but to others, he is a beacon, a steady presence in the storm, offering guidance when the way forward seems unclear. His light shines not in grand gestures but in the simple, heartfelt moments—in the way he listens, the way he cares, the way his very presence brings comfort. And yet, I wish he could truly understand the depth of his own strength, the quiet power that radiates from him. He doesn't realize the healing found in his embrace or the steady reassurance in his voice when he pulls me close and whispers, "You are so strong. You got this." If only he saw what I see—the unwavering resilience, the depth of his love, the way his soul carries a gentleness that transforms those around him. He is stronger than he knows, more powerful than he believes, and more loved than he could ever imagine.

Our older daughter wrestles against the relentless weight of past mistakes, longing to grasp the truth of how profoundly she is loved. She can't see herself through the eyes of God—the powerful, radiant soul she is when her heart finds refuge in Him. Yet even as she carries the burden of her own struggles, she reaches for others, extending compassion with quiet strength, lifting up the wounded and standing fiercely for the forgotten. It will be within her own pain that she discovers a calling—not in spite of her suffering, but because of it. She will become a refuge for the broken, a beacon for those who have lost their way. She carries a strength that is undeniable, a will that stands firm, a resilience that doesn't waver. She is fierce in conviction, unwavering in purpose, and determined in spirit. Yet beneath that tough exterior beats a heart of immeasurable depth, a love so steadfast and true that it defies expectations. Her love isn't fleeting or shallow; it's rooted, enduring. She feels deeply, loves fiercely and gives wholly. While the world may see her as tough, those who know her understand that her greatest power lies within the tenderness she so carefully guards. When she loves, she loves with everything—without hesitation, without pretense, without condition. She is both iron and warmth, both protector and nurturer. And in that balance of fortitude and grace, she carries a love that is as unshakable as her will—a love that, like her, stands the test of time. It simply exists—steady, unwavering, speaking volumes in the smallest of gestures. Gestures that support her dad and me, gestures she doesn't realize lift our spirits. And though she continues to face difficult trials in her journey toward wholeness, she carries a strength that's both humbling and extraordinary. In moments when my own heart wavers, she steadies me with the simplest yet most profound words: "You are my best friend." Although she feels she is too broken to love; her dad and I love every piece of her.

Our youngest daughter is a radiant soul—tender-hearted, deeply emotional, and overflowing with a love that knows no bounds. She cherishes her family with a devotion that is both fierce and unwavering, a loyalty that wraps around us like the softest embrace. There is an intensity to her love that is neither overwhelming nor possessive, but rather, profoundly comforting and endlessly inspiring. Her devotion to her dad and me is steadfast, a bond woven with the purest affection. Whether she is sharing her joys with contagious excitement, seeking solace in moments of uncertainty, or simply checking in with thoughtful tenderness, her presence is a beacon of light that brightens even the dullest of days. She carries the best of her father—his quick wit, his effortless charm, his unshakable grace. She brings laughter like a warm breeze, lightening even the heaviest moments with humor that is both clever and infectious. But beyond her playful spirit lies a quiet poise, a grace that moves through her like an unspoken strength. She navigates life with a balance of joy and wisdom, always knowing when to lift others up with laughter and when to offer steady reassurance. In her, humor and grace are not separate qualities—they intertwine, creating a presence that is both radiant and deeply comforting. She carries the ability to love in a way that transforms ordinary moments into cherished memories. To be loved by her is to know a depth of care that is unshaken, a kindness that touches the soul. Every moment spent with her is a reminder that love, in its truest form, is both gentle and powerful, unassuming yet profound. Although she sometimes struggles with feeling alone because of her shyness, I hope she always remembers that her dad and I will always be by her side—and that we love her deeply.

Life has shaped each of them in ways words cannot fully capture. Though we tried to shield them from suffering, they knew. They felt the weight of it all. And yet, through every hardship, they have stood tall, bending but never breaking beneath the force of life's relentless trials. There were moments when doubt crept in, when the weight seemed unbearable—but time and again, they found their footing, clinging to the unwavering truth that God is always working.

As a parent, the depth of my love aches within me. Every fiber of my being longs to take away their suffering, to carry their burdens as my own. I have prayed the desperate prayer, "Lord, let this cup pass from them." I would give anything to bear their pain, to shield them from sorrow. And yet, I know—they must walk through this fire, for it is shaping them, refining them, strengthening them in ways I cannot fully comprehend. I understand it, but oh, how it pains me to watch.

So, I sit in the quiet, lifting them up in prayer, trusting that God is guiding their steps—even when the road is unclear. The storm will pass. And when it does, they will emerge stronger, their spirits fortified by the trials they have endured. No matter what comes, they will always have parents who stand unwavering in prayer—wrapping them in unconditional love.

Perhaps, this is how God sees us—His beloved, struggling through the trials of life. He understands our frailty, He sees our silent tears, and yet His love remains steady, unchanging. In the depths of our sorrow, He whispers, *"You will make it through. Hold onto Me."*

Brokenness—it's a word that often carries an air of tragedy... an ache... a sense of loss. We recoil at the thought of shattered things, fractured bones, splintered dreams. But what if brokenness wasn't the end? What if, instead of ruin, it led to redemption?

Did you know that when a bone breaks, it doesn't simply heal—it rebuilds itself stronger than before? What was once fragile becomes fortified. Spiritual breaking isn't the end, it's the beginning. If you've ever suffered a broken bone, your first instinct is pain—deep, searing, undeniable pain. The healing process is slow, difficult, and sometimes agonizing. Yet just as a skilled surgeon aligns a fracture for proper healing, God works through our broken places—not to destroy us, but to transform us into something more resilient, radiant, and refined.

This truth became profoundly real during one of our children's revivals—a night when brokenness took center stage in the most unexpected way. After the service, my husband and I sat down to discuss the lesson for the following night. An unease stirred within me—an unshakable sense that the lesson plan needed to change. My husband hesitated, unconvinced. But deep within, I knew God was setting something in motion. And then, it happened. As he began teaching the next night on brokenness, the unpredictable unfolded—my husband gashed his hand on a

184

lightbulb. The wound was deep, and blood spilled freely, unbidden, pooling in his palm. Shocked, he blurted out, "Um, Sunflower, I need help." That single phrase sent a ripple of alarm through me. This wasn't planned. It wasn't staged. It was real. Bounding through the curtain, I saw the raw panic etched across his face as I noticed his back was to the audience. Something in me tightened—this was not how the night was supposed to go. But there was no time for hesitation; we had to act. Covering our shock, we wove humor into the moment, cracking jokes to keep the atmosphere light as we worked to slow the bleeding. We made laughter our shield, though inside, we questioned everything. Even the pastor's wife was convinced it was part of the act, laughing hysterically as if this had all been rehearsed. But it wasn't. Wayne and I knew this was supposed to be a solemn lesson on brokenness. Yet here we were—stumbling through a moment that felt messy, chaotic, and utterly off-script. Was this truly what God intended?

And then, revelation. Just as a glow stick must be bent and broken before it can shine, our souls must endure seasons of breaking before the fullness of our anointing can be released. The very fractures we fear... are the ones through which His light breaks forth. And just as that truth settled in my heart, the doors at the back of the sanctuary creaked open. A man and his girlfriend stepped inside, arriving just as the altar call began. Their presence carried weight—a heaviness that lingered in the air. Though they had missed the lesson, their eyes spoke volumes. The young man fought to suppress his emotions, but no matter how tightly he held them back, they surged forward, overwhelming him. He stood abruptly, tears brimming, and ran to the altar. His girlfriend remained frozen—torn between the urge to follow him and the chains of hesitation wrapped around her heart. Standing behind the curtain watching this unfold, I felt a pang of disappointment. Had they arrived only moments earlier, they would have heard the very words God had prepared for them. Then, softly, God whispered: "Take a glow stick and go to her. Be My voice." That single instruction shifted everything. Suddenly, I understood—she didn't need the sermon from the pulpit. She needed something deeper, something personal. God was calling me to minister to her one-on-one, to reach her heart in a way that a sermon never could.

What I didn't know was that God was speaking the same thought to the pastor concerning the young man. Just moments earlier, the young man had confessed, "God can't use me. I am broken." But he didn't yet understand the profound truth: His brokenness wasn't a burden, it was his greatest gift. How often do we resist brokenness—forgetting that it's the very soil from which beauty blooms?

The Lord is close to the brokenhearted and saves those who are crushed in spirit.—Psalm 34:18 NIV

Through the different seasons of my life, I've learned one powerful truth—I've never felt closer to the Lord than in my deepest moments of brokenness. Rather than leaving us shattered, He uses the breaking to free us—to break away the fears, the doubts, the limitations we place upon ourselves. The process is rarely gentle: It is painful, unpredictable and can be overwhelming. But if we yield to His hand, we will find that He doesn't leave us in pieces. Instead, He molds us into something greater. That night, as I spoke to the young woman, I saw it—a flicker of hope igniting in her eyes, piercing through the sorrow. And I wonder... does God feel the same satisfaction when He watches us rise from our brokenness?

There is beauty in brokenness—a beauty where the light of Jesus shines through the cracks we once tried to conceal. Even when we can't see Him, feel Him, or hear Him—He is working. The darkness is not an end—it is the perfect backdrop for His brilliance.

Consider the glow stick—a simple, unassuming vessel that holds the potential for brilliance. Within it, two compounds lie dormant, waiting. But until it is shaken, bent, and broken, it remains lifeless, dim. Only in surrender—only in the breaking—does it unleash its radiance.

Our lives are much the same. We often settle for flickers, for shadows of what we were meant to be, when God has called us to burn bright, to be beacons of His love, His truth, His glory. The trials that shake us, the hardships that bend us, the moments that threaten to break us—they are not meant to destroy us. They are meant to reveal the brilliance placed within us all along.

Perhaps, in the pressing, in the shaking, God is preparing you for something greater. He wastes nothing—not a single wound, not a single tear. If we trust Him, He will use every shattered piece for good, transforming what feels broken into a light that cannot be dimmed.

Becoming God's glow stick isn't easy. But you already hold within you everything necessary to shine. And the more bending, shaking, and breaking you endure, the brighter His light will blaze through you. So do not resist the bends of life—this is your moment... this is your calling.

There is blessing in brokenness. And when the world around you grows dark, that is precisely when His light in you will shine the brightest.

Eleven: In the Midst of the Pain

Where Suffering Meets Purpose

The previous chapters may have felt like the final pages of a long and arduous journey. But our story is far from over—it continues with every breath we take. Now is the time to rise above doubt, pain, and fear and declare the testimony God has given us.

They triumphed over him by the blood of the Lamb and by the word of their testimony; they did not love their lives so much as to shrink from death.—Revelation 12:11 NIV

Each of us carries a testimony—but who among us is truly willing to speak of the shadows we've walked through, the battles that nearly broke us? The very word *testimony* begins with *test*—but how many are willing to endure the refining fire in order to emerge with a testimony worthy of His name?

We dream of doing great things for God, but do we fully grasp the price of ministry? It may not always require suffering, but it will require faith in the midst of trials. It's through tribulation that we learn to trust. It is through hardship that we learn to listen for His voice. It is through brokenness that we learn to walk where He leads—no matter how treacherous the path ahead.

Those who know our family will tell you—our life has been a tapestry woven with trials, each strand a moment of testing, each knot a lesson learned. At first, it felt as though God had singled us out—placing weight upon our shoulders that we could hardly bear. From the outside, many struggled to understand. But looking back, we see His hand in every step. We see the refinement, the preparation, the divine orchestration shaping us for what was to come.

> *See, I have refined you, though not as silver; I have tested you in the furnace of affliction.*—Isaiah 48:10 NIV

The *furnace of affliction*—the words alone conjure visions of searing flames, of trials that threaten to consume. It's a crucible—unrelenting and unforgiving—yet designed not to destroy, but to refine. And when you realize you were *chosen* in that furnace, everything changes. It's no longer aimless suffering or meaningless pain. It becomes *purposeful*. It's a shaping, a molding, a divine work unfolding in the heat of hardship.

190

Looking back, I could have chosen to be swallowed by sorrow, to let despair wrap itself around me like a suffocating shroud. I could have surrendered to bitterness, clung to resentment as if it were a shield. But what did resentment ever produce? Nothing. It bore no fruit, it offered no healing, it provided no redemption, it offered no peace. I refused to let pain be the author of my story. Instead, I choose to see the beauty He has woven from the ashes. I choose to lift my eyes and behold the masterpiece He is crafting—born from agony, shaped by fire, but destined for glory.

Some family members questioned how I could ever possibly forgive those who had inflicted such deep pain. To them, forgiveness was unthinkable—a concept beyond reason, beyond reach. But forgiveness isn't a dismissal of the wounds; it doesn't erase the scars or invalidate the pain. *Forgiveness is freedom.* It the key that unlocks the suffocating grip of bitterness, unshackling the soul from resentment's heavy chains so the soul can breathe again.

The purpose of my first book was never to cast judgment, never to shame, never to expose. It was to illuminate—to reveal the undeniable, unwavering presence of God and His mercy that reaches into the darkest depths. It was about His restoration that breathes life into places declared too broken to repair; His healing power that mends what was once shattered beyond recognition.

Many doubted that I could move forward in faith after everything I had endured. Truthfully, I doubted it too. I questioned whether trust could ever live again in a heart so torn. It wasn't easy. It was excruciating. But it was possible—because *He* made it possible.

Unforgiveness is a poison—a slow, strangling toxin that seeps into the soul, corrupting the heart with resentment, anger, and sorrow. It consumes, it festers, it chains. It clouds judgment, twists truth, and replaces healing with rage. Why would I choose such a fate? Why would I willingly carry a burden that was never mine to bear? So instead, I surrendered my pain to Jesus. I laid it at His feet—trembling, exhausted, undone. And in that surrender, I found something I had been missing for far too long: *Peace*.

And when that peace finally came, it wasn't just for me. I didn't rejoice only in my own freedom. My heart wept for the ones who had inflicted suffering upon me. I wept for the souls still held captive, for those trapped in cycles they couldn't escape.

To this day, some of them remain bound—shackled to the very shadows they once cast upon me. They walk through life imprisoned by their own choices, tormented by the very demons they once unleashed. If only they would turn to Jesus. If only they would surrender—not in shame, but in redemption. But instead, they remain adrift. Isolated. Haunted by regret. And until they release their burdens at His feet, until they allow grace to pierce through the darkness…their sorrow will remain unshaken.

And here's a truth that may be difficult for some to grasp: If given the choice, I would walk through it all again—every trial, every wound, every moment of despair—if it meant becoming who I am today. Because today, I stand redeemed. I'm not just someone who survived—I am a child of God—transformed through the very pain that once tried to destroy me. My testimony is not a tale of defeat; it's a declaration of His unwavering grace, His unfailing love, His boundless restoration.

That fire I walked through—the one I believed would break me—it didn't. It revealed what had always been true: Jesus had never left my side. In the midst of the agony, when I felt abandoned, He was there—steady, faithful, guiding me through the haze of my suffering.

Looking back now, I can see the hardships with clarity. Yet in that moment, I was drowning in emotion—overwhelmed by grief, blinded by sorrow. I never imagined I would someday call my abusive past a *blessing*. But I do. Not because of the pain itself, but because of the redemption that followed, because of the healing He provided, the strength He forged and the victory He declared over my life.

And that victory wasn't just for me. It is for the ones still searching—still hurting—still desperate to find light in the middle of their darkness. That is why I speak, why I testify, why I stand unshaken—because what He has done in me, He can do

193

for others. He is not finished—not with me—not with them—not with *you*.

I'll never forget the woman at my book signing. Her eyes brimmed with tears, her voice trembling with urgency as she leapt across the table and cried, "Your book saved my life!" Those words are forever etched into my soul. They remind me this journey was never just about me—it became a *ministry*. A ministry born from ashes... yet blooming with grace.

I don't wish to slip into Heaven quietly, by the skin of my salvation. No—I want to storm the Gates of Glory with an army. An army of souls who found hope, healing, and eternal life because I said yes to His call. Souls touched, restored, and redeemed—not by my power, but by the hand of Almighty God.

If we're not careful, anger becomes a thief—a silent predator lurking in the shadows of our past, waiting for the perfect moment to strike. It consumes our thoughts, distorts our reality, and wraps its cold fingers around our hearts, whispering lies that keep us chained to wounds long since inflicted. We become prisoners—not to the pain itself, but to the weight of our own unforgiveness.

Don't misunderstand—abuse is a tragedy, an injustice that should never be excused. What happened to me was cruel, and those who should have stood for truth instead turned away, pretending they didn't see. But here's what I've learned: I can't rewrite history. I can't undo the pain. The past is sewn into the fabric of my story, and no amount of rage, sorrow, or regret will erase it. But here's the truth: The past *doesn't* get to dictate the future. There comes a moment—a crossroads where we must make a choice. Do we remain tethered to the weight of yesterday, or do we rise? Every sunrise offers an invitation, an opportunity to choose something greater. I chose to silence the anger that had gripped me for too long. I refused to let pain become the author of my story. I decided my past would no longer pursue me, no longer control me, or suffocate me. *I chose joy. I chose freedom. I chose Jesus.*

I laid my anguish at His feet, surrendered my brokenness into His hands, and in return, He clothed me in peace. I refused to settle for a life spent merely *existing*. I wanted *more*. I craved wholeness. I desired transformation. The only difference between *bitter* and *better* is a single letter—*"I."* And *I* chose better.

The enemy watches, waiting for weakness, searching for cracks in the armor. He thrives on deception, weaving memories of past suffering into carefully crafted illusions. He whispers the wounds back into existence, resurrecting shadows that threaten to darken the light. But God—steadfast, sovereign, and true— stands between me and the past, declaring what the enemy fears most: *"The truth shall set you free."* And freedom is the one thing the enemy can't withstand.

Perhaps you wonder, what is this wholeness you speak of? How does it differ from healing?

Let's take a journey into Scripture—a moment not just of restoration, but of something far deeper:

Now on his way to Jerusalem, Jesus traveled along the border between Samaria and Galilee. As he was going into a village, ten men who had leprosy met him. They stood at a distance and called out in a loud voice, "Jesus, Master, have pity on us!" When he saw them, he said, "Go, show yourselves to the priests." And as they went, they were cleansed. One of them, when he saw he was healed, came back, praising God in a loud voice. He threw himself at Jesus' feet and thanked him—and he was a Samaritan. Jesus asked, "Were not all ten cleansed? Where are the other nine? Has no one returned to give praise to God except this foreigner?" Then he said to him, "Rise and go; your faith has made you well.—Luke 17:11–19 NIV

Ten were healed. But only one was *made whole*. Healing cleanses the wound, wholeness restores the soul (body); healing removes affliction; wholeness redefines your spiritual identity.

The nine received their miracle—but only *one* returned, filled with gratitude, overflowing with reverence, faith ignited beyond the physical—spiritual restoration. And it was his faith that made him whole.

Many seek healing—an end to suffering, a release from torment. And healing *is* a gift from God, an undeniable expression of His mercy. But healing is only the *beginning*. Wholeness is something greater, something deeper. Wholeness is stepping beyond relief and into transformation. It doesn't just soothe pain—it gives purpose to it. It doesn't just cleanse the wound—it rewrites the story. Wholeness is not merely surviving the fire. It's emerging *refined* by it. And that is the difference, that is the promise, that is the victory of God.

Leprosy—an affliction steeped in fear and sorrow—was more than a disease; it was a life sentence of isolation, despair, and abandonment. It stripped men and women of their dignity, their families, their very identity, leaving them as mere shadows of who they once were. Those marked by leprosy bore not only the visible scars of disfigurement but the invisible wounds of rejection. Their skin, once smooth and whole, became marred with wounds. Their limbs grew weak, numb to pain yet never numb to suffering. The loss of feeling meant that injuries worsened, infections spread, and slowly, pieces of themselves— once taken for granted—were lost forever and died. But worse than the physical agony was the silence—the unbearable separation from the world they knew. They were banished, forgotten, declared *unclean*.

The ten lepers had lived that reality, their days void of human touch. Their nights haunted by unanswered prayers. They had no future—only survival. And then... Jesus. Word of Him had spread—stories of miraculous healings, sight restored to the blind, strength returning to the lame. Hope flickered in the hearts of these ten men as they saw Him from a distance. Could He do for them what He had done for others? The chance was too precious to waste, so they cried out—not with polished words, but with raw desperation, lifting their voices above the crowd, above the weight of their suffering. *"Jesus, Master, have mercy on us!"* It wasn't a demand. It was a plea—a desperate call from souls who had exhausted every other hope. They didn't ask for riches, status, or favor. They simply wanted mercy and Jesus answered. But not as expected; He didn't touch them, reassure them, or explain. Instead, He gave a simple command: *"Go, show yourselves to the priests."* It was a test of faith. The priests held the power to declare them clean, yet their bodies were still afflicted. Would they go? Would they believe before they saw? Without hesitation, they went. And somewhere along the way, the miracle happened—the disease transformed, their skin restored, and the pain lifted. Imagine their joy—their disbelief— their laughter and shouts of astonishment. *They were healed!* Yet amid the celebration, something unexpected happened: nine pressed forward, eager to rejoin the world they had lost—but one stopped. One understood that healing wasn't the greatest gift— *Wholeness* was. And wholeness could only be found in the presence of the One who had healed him. He turned back, heart pounding, eyes filled with tears. How could he not? How could he rush forward without first returning to bow before Jesus? He knew—deep within—that this moment was greater than any reunion, greater than any homecoming. He had encountered the living God. Falling at Jesus" feet, he worshiped. His gratitude was boundless, undignified, overflowing, uncontainable. And Jesus noticed. *"Were not ten cleansed? Where are the other nine?"* Jesus didn't ask because He needed recognition. He asked because He had something greater to give—something beyond the physical. Nine received healing, but only one received *wholeness.*

What about us today? Have we settled for mere blessings when God longs to shape us, refine us, transform us into something far beyond what we imagined? Do we cry out in desperation—hands lifted in pleading—only to let gratitude slip through our fingers the moment the answer arrives?

If Jesus granted every prayer exactly as we asked, could we unknowingly rob ourselves of something greater? Would we choose relief over revelation, comfort over calling? God is never confined, never restrained, never lacking. Yet how often do we impose limitations upon Him with the smallness of our vision, the narrowness of our faith? We see only the moment—the urgent need, the immediate longing—while He beholds the grand tapestry, the unseen threads that weave together destiny, redemption, and wholeness. So what is the posture of our hearts? Do we approach Him with expectation, with humility, with reverence? Or have we unknowingly adopted an attitude of entitlement, of indifference, of silent resignation?

The ten lepers understood desperation. They knew suffering intimately—their days marked by loneliness, rejection, loss. They cried out, they obeyed, they received their healing. Yet only one turned back. Only one saw beyond his physical restoration and recognized the deeper invitation—not just a touch of cleansing, but a touch of completion. Imagine for a moment, the nine who pressed forward—eager to reenter society, to embrace family, to reclaim the life they had lost. Then imagine the moment they saw the one who had returned to Jesus—the one who had been made whole. Did they feel a pang of regret? Did they wonder, in some quiet moment, if they had missed something far greater than healing? We don't blame them for their eagerness. Their suffering had been relentless, their exile cruel. And yet, only one understood the truth—*true restoration is never found in returning to what was, but in returning to Jesus.*

Was it easy for him? No. His heart must have ached for home, for the embrace of familiar comforts. But he saw what the others had missed: he understood that Jesus had not authored his pain—He had answered it. And in that sacred moment, as he fell at the feet of his Redeemer, his spirit erupted in joy: *"I am whole! I am whole!"* This is what Jesus desires for you: —not merely healing, not simply answered prayers, not just restoration—but wholeness. Yet how often do we stop short? How often do we settle for less, believing the miracle is complete when Jesus is still reaching toward something deeper?

I will never forget the night my healing came: —the weight that lifted, the flood of peace that washed over me like a rushing river. I remember the room, the atmosphere thick with the presence of God. The words spoken that night are imprinted on my soul. In that moment, I thought I had tasted the fullness of joy—but there was more. There was something beyond the relief, beyond the restoration, beyond the beautiful satisfaction of healing. I didn't understand it then—but I see it now: *my suffering was not wasted.* It was not random; it was not meaningless. It was a passage, a refining fire, a preparation for something I couldn't yet comprehend.

Not everyone reaches that revelation. Some remain bound—hesitant to turn back and give thanks, unable to reconcile the idea that pain could ever be a gift. And yet, *when healing becomes wholeness, a choice is born: the choice to surrender, to release, to allow God to use what once broke us for His glory.*

I will never forget the moment I fell to my knees, my face buried in trembling hands, as tears poured freely from a place deep within. And in that moment, I did the unthinkable—I thanked the Lord for every hardship, every trial, every wound. I thanked Him for carrying me when I couldn't stand, for turning my mourning into a ministry, for transforming the ashes into beauty. Something shifted. A river of refreshing swept through my soul, filling every empty space, healing every fractured piece. I was changed, my anger—gone, the bitterness—lifted, the weight of sorrow—released. I was clean. And before I knew it, Jesus had done what only He could do—He had made me whole. My spirit cried out, *"Thank you, Jesus!"* And in that moment, I understood mercy. I understood grace. I understood love in its purest, most powerful form.

Perhaps you're not there yet. Perhaps the pain still grips you, the wounds still ache, the silence still echoes. I understand. *I see you.* I know the weight you carry—the long nights, the unanswered questions. For years, I lived in that space—fists clenched, heart hardened, silent cries for help filling the space between who I was and who I longed to be. I walked in a fog of frustration, believing the world owed me something, demanding explanations for the suffering that marked my story. *Why me? Why my family? Why this battle?* Those questions trapped me, bound me to a cycle of despair. The enemy whispered lies— *"You will never heal." "You are broken beyond repair."* And I believed him. But that's what the adversary does, he crafts illusions. The merry-go-round syndrome: movement that masquerades as progress, a never-ending cycle that deceives the weary soul into thinking change is coming while it only spins them deeper into sorrow. A cycle of motion without progress, exhaustion without freedom. Healing is a choice. Stepping forward—even when your feet tremble—is a choice. Believing that God is working, even when we don't see it, is a choice.

The ten lepers took that step of faith before their healing had even manifested and so must we. At first glance, their story may seem like one of gratitude. But look deeper—it's about endurance, obedience, and redemption. It's about embracing not just healing, but wholeness—the kind that transforms pain into purpose. Wholeness doesn't simply restore—it empowers. It enables us to say, "I understand. I've walked that road. I've carried that pain." It emboldens us to speak through our scars, believing that God can use even the deepest wounds for His glory. And when that happens—pain is no longer an affliction; it becomes an offering. Tears are no longer a sign of weakness— they are a testament to redemption.

It's in the fire of our trials that we are refined, shaped, and made whole. But gratitude—true, deep gratitude—isn't easy in a world that fosters entitlement, a world that whispers, *"You are owed."* This world thrives on entitlement.
It feeds on offense. It worships the illusion of fairness. We are not owed anything. Sympathy may feel comforting, but it does not equal truth. Only the Word of God holds that authority.

The world will eagerly detour your path, but His way leads to life. It is time to turn back—not with reluctance or shame, but with gratitude. Jesus loves you. He desires for you to find that sacred place where pain becomes a tool, not a torment—a tool that, if surrendered, will minister in ways beyond your imagination.

Can you see the difference the tenth leper made? The testimony that rippled through generations? *That story still speaks today.* I, too, want a heart of gratitude—not just for the easy blessings, but for everything Jesus does in my life, whether I perceive it as good or bad. Go ahead. Bow before Him. Let your prayers be saturated in thanksgiving. It will change the way you think, align your heart with His will, and usher in the wholeness your soul longs for.

Spiritual thankfulness is a sacred posture of the soul: an unwavering acknowledgment that every moment, every trial, and every triumph is woven into the divine masterpiece of God's design. It is not merely gratitude for blessings, but a deep, abiding trust that His wisdom far exceeds our understanding. It means praising Him in abundance and in scarcity, in joy and in sorrow, knowing that even the fiercest storms are held within His sovereign hands. This thankfulness doesn't waver in uncertainty, nor does it diminish in suffering. It flourishes, rooting itself in the eternal promise that *God is good*—not because of what He gives, but because of who He is.

And when the heart embraces this truth, gratitude becomes worship—transforming our perspective from longing for what is missing to celebrating the overwhelming presence of His unfailing love. It is the quiet surrender in which you whisper, *"Lord, I trust You. I thank You. Not for what You have done alone, but for who You are. And that is enough."*

Twelve: Be the One

Answering the Unspoken Cry

*H*ave you ever closed the final page of a book and felt a lingering ache—wondering what became of its characters long after the story ended? Their journey doesn't stop when the ink dries. It lingers—threading itself through your thoughts, urging reflection, inviting you to question, to dream, to wonder.

When I completed my first book over two decades ago, I stood at the threshold of what I thought was certainty. I believed, with unwavering conviction, that I understood God's plan for my life—His purpose, His calling, His will. But how naïve I was. I barely grasped the profound intricacy of His design.

The path He laid before me was anything but predictable. It wasn't the smooth road I'd envisioned, but a tempest—wild, unrelenting, breathtaking in its fury. It was a battle that demanded every ounce of courage I could muster. A refining fire that stripped away the illusions I had clung to, burning away self-reliance and pride until all that remained was surrender. The storms were fierce, the roads impossibly long, and the lessons carved not gently—but with relentless precision—into the marrow of my soul.

Yet, as I stand in the clarity of hindsight, I see His fingerprints upon every moment, and how every hardship bore His presence. Every victory echoed His grace, but amid the storm, I was blind—caught in the chaos, ensnared by regrets, yearning for a surrender I had yet to offer. How often did I grip the reins with trembling hands, convinced that control was mine to hold? How often did I shrink beneath the weight of fear when faith was the only true refuge?

Looking back, I know this: His plan was never about the path I expected—it was always about the transformation happening within me. And though I once wished I had surrendered sooner, trusted deeper, walked boldly rather than hesitantly—I now understand. Every struggle, every tear, every moment of doubt was shaping me into the person He always intended me to become.

And so, I wrote this book with one fervent prayer: That you will step boldly—without hesitation—into the fullness of what God has prepared for you. That you will not merely wait, hoping for change, but instead rise with unwavering resolve and *be* the change.

The enemy seeks to entangle your spirit in the shadows of doubt—to whisper deception until it feels like truth, to shackle you in fear and hesitation. But you were not made for chains. You were made for freedom. Refuse to let him dictate your steps, cast off his lies, silence his distractions. Break free from every snare that threatens to hold you captive.

Run—without fear, without hesitation—into the boundless, unwavering embrace of Jesus. Run as though your soul already knows the way, as though the weight has lifted, as though victory is already yours—because it is.

Understand this: The enemy's greatest weapon is delay. If he can keep your heart tangled in uncertainty—if he can plant seeds of doubt that steal your courage—he can weaken your resolve. But *you* are designed for more. You are called to walk boldly, to stand unshaken, to chase after the purpose God has placed within you—without delay, without regret, without surrendering to fear. *Now* is the time. *Now* is the moment. Step forward—step fully into the life God has written for you.

Far too often, we shrink beneath the weight of our circumstances, losing sight of the greater story being written. We focus inward, drowning in our struggles, when in truth, it's our own resistance—our own hesitation—that stands in the way. We must shift our gaze—away from the problem and toward the limitless power of the One who has already overcome. There is absolutely nothing too difficult for the Lord. It's not the magnitude of our obstacles—it's our reluctance to relinquish control. It's time to lay down pride, fear, and doubt, and recognize that we are not meant to carry this burden alone. God's wisdom stretches beyond our limited understanding; His plans are far greater than anything we could conceive, and His ways—though sometimes mysterious—are always perfect.

Have you grown weary of merely holding the line, of standing guard while the battle rages? I know I have. It's time to stop bracing for the next attack and rise. No more retreat. No more hesitation. The enemy has taken enough—he has stolen, deceived, and dismantled what is rightfully ours, but no more.

We are not victims—we are warriors, commissioned to stand, called to fight, and anointed to reclaim what was lost. We carry the authority of Heaven, the power of God's promises, and the strength of His unfailing presence. And when Jesus leads the way, victory is a certainty, not a mere hope.

We've lingered in the shadows long enough. Fear has silenced too many voices. Doubt has paralyzed too many hearts. But the time for waiting is over. The call to rise is now.

Go forth—not timidly, but boldly. Stand—not in defeat, but in divine confidence. Move—not cautiously, but with unrelenting faith. The battle belongs to the Lord, and with Him, we do not simply survive—we overcome. The enemy may roar, but he is already defeated. So let him tremble—because we *will* take back what is ours.

Over the years, I've watched my family walk through fires that could have consumed us, battling unseen forces that threatened to shake our foundation, and emerge not unscathed, but stronger. We didn't break, nor did we surrender to despair. And through every storm, we discovered this truth again and again: grace isn't found in the absence of struggle—but in the courage to endure.

My four children now have families of their own, embarking on their own journeys, forging their own legacies. And though we were far from perfect parents—though we stumbled, doubted, and made mistakes—they saw something unshakable. We didn't give up. We didn't cower when the winds howled, nor did we let failure define us. We fought. We persevered. We chose faith over fear, and determination over defeat.

My prayer is that they carry this truth with them—not just the lessons learned from our mistakes but the unwavering resolve we clung to when the road seemed impossible. That they come to understand life isn't measured by perfection but by an unyielding commitment to rise, to press forward, to stand firm even when everything around them tries to take them down.

The enemy thrives on doubt, fear, and condemnation. He whispers reminders of failures, hoping to bind us to our regrets—hoping to drown us in hesitation. But his chains lose their grip when we stop listening and when we stand on the promises of God. And when we choose to believe that we were never meant to live in defeat—we were meant to overcome.

So, let this truth sink deep: *You are not defined by your failures.* You are not disqualified because of your missteps. As long as you have breath, you still have the opportunity to rise again. Today is a new beginning. Take it one step at a time. Keep moving... Keep striving... Keep pressing into Jesus. He hears you—*yes, He hears you!* And He stands ready—arms open wide—waiting for you to surrender, to trust, to embrace His love. He will never force His way into your life, but He longs for relationship. He will never leave you. He will never forsake you. He knows your every need... even before you speak it.

Looking back, I see it clearly now—Jesus knew exactly what I needed in a husband. Long before I understood the battles I'd face, the trials that would refine me, the storms that would shake my spirit... He was already preparing the perfect partner to stand beside me. And even now, I marvel at how masterfully He orchestrated it all.

My husband is a man of unwavering patience, boundless love, and quiet, steady wisdom—the kind that anchors me when the winds howl and the waves rise. When weariness settles deep in my bones, when frustration grips my spirit, I find refuge in his presence. He isn't just a companion; he's a pillar. A foundation God placed in my life to remind me I'm never alone in the battle. I don't always understand how he carries such strength, how he speaks peace into chaos, how he knows exactly when to stand firm and when to simply be, but he does. And he knows me— knows that I am a fighter—a woman who prays with tenacity, who refuses to surrender, whose confidence is rooted in the unshakable promises of God.

Together, Jesus knew we would be the perfect fit for the ministry He envisioned—long before we ever saw it for ourselves. Before we knew our calling... before we grasped the depth of our purpose... He was weaving our strengths together—binding our hearts with passion, our hands with service, and our voices with truth. And when the time was right, He breathed life into this ministry—a sacred work where we became Handy Dandy and Sunflower.

Time and again, people approach us and say, "This ministry isn't just for children—it touches everyone." And they're right. Jesus knew all along what He was crafting. Every trial, every setback, every heartbreak was shaping something greater than we could've imagined. It wasn't punishment—it was preparation. It was the refining of gifts, the sharpening of purpose, the unfolding of a masterpiece only He could see from the beginning. We could've succumbed to bitterness, let doubt overshadow hope, allowed weariness to silence our calling. But we chose faith. Again and again—we chose faith. We chose to trust that He was working all things together for His good. The road was grueling, marked with failures, laced with moments where it felt impossible to rise. But each time we fell, we found strength—*not in ourselves,* but in the One who lifts, restores, and redeems.

And now, as I stand in the clarity of hindsight, I see it—every step, every scar, every victory was written by the hand of a God who never abandoned us for a single moment.

I will be the first to admit—I've stumbled, I've doubted. I've made choices that left me standing in the wreckage, asking myself, *"What was I thinking?"* There were moments when I ached to be seen—truly seen. For someone to peer past the walls I'd built, to reach into the depths of my heart, to understand the silent battles I was too afraid to voice. But I was terrified. Vulnerability felt like surrender... and surrender felt like weakness.

I wanted someone to pull me into the light, to rescue me from the shadows, to lift me from the weight of my own uncertainty. But that isn't how God works. He doesn't simply pluck us from the fire—He walks into it *with* us. He doesn't force the walls to crumble—He waits, patiently, for us to trust Him enough to let them down. He moves, not through grand, dramatic rescues, but in quiet whispers, gentle nudges, and through the hearts of the people He has placed around us.

And I know—sometimes, that feels impossible. Trust can feel fragile. Reaching out can feel like a risk too great to take. But God never asks us to walk alone. He never designed us for isolation. He calls us to lean in—to let Him work through the very relationships He has woven into our lives, even when doubt lingers, even when fear tries to take hold.

And when we finally find the strength to rise—when we surrender the weight we were never meant to carry alone—we discover something greater than rescue. We find redemption, we find healing, we find *Him*.

As a child, I endured severe mental, physical, and sexual abuse—wounds that didn't just mark my body but carved themselves into my spirit. The scars ran deep, shaping my fears, my silence, my rage. I was trapped in a battle I never chose, carrying burdens no child should ever bear. I couldn't understand why no one saw, why no one noticed the bruises—not just the ones that blemished my skin, but the ones that darkened my heart. Why no one noticed the shift, the quiet unraveling, the pain carefully tucked behind my eyes. Did they believe this was simply who I was? That my struggle, my anger, my retreat into silence were part of my nature—and not my cry for help? I never wanted to be difficult. I was drowning and all I wanted—*all I needed*—was an escape.

Yet even then—when I felt most alone, most unseen, most abandoned—*God was there.* In the moments where despair whispered that I was forgotten, He saw me. When fear told me I was beyond saving, He knew my pain. When the weight of sorrow threatened to consume me, He held me.

Healing didn't come quickly. It didn't erase the past or magically undo the suffering. It came in layers—in quiet moments of surrender, in hesitant steps toward restoration I could barely bring myself to take. But *He* led me—tenderly, patiently—toward freedom. Toward the life I thought had been stolen, toward the purpose that pain couldn't destroy.

And now, as I stand in the aftermath—not broken, but restored—I know this: My story is not one of ruin, it's one of redemption.

My anger was never meant to be destructive. It was a manifestation of a desperate struggle to make sense of circumstances far beyond my control.

One night, after enduring yet another sexual assault at the hands of my stepfather, the anger inside me erupted. I couldn't bear it any longer. In desperation, I crawled through my bedroom window and ran—screaming—releasing every emotion raging within me. I ran faster and faster, my feet pounding against the earth, until exhaustion overtook and I collapsed, miles from home. Injured and bleeding, I scanned my surroundings for shelter. A few feet away, I spotted a dark, cold concrete culvert. Though I recognized the potential dangers, knowing that remaining exposed posed an even greater threat, I moved forward. The culvert granted me a fleeting illusion of safety, a fragile refuge amid chaos. I wasn't sure why, but at that moment, I felt something I hadn't in a long time: A sliver of peace.

Eventually, sleep embraced me, cradled by the gentle symphony of nature—a whispered lullaby carried on the rustling leaves, interwoven with the rhythmic chorus of distant crickets. Time dissolved into the night, and when I awoke, the world was swallowed by an oppressive darkness, thick and absolute. The void outside mirrored the hollow ache within me—a labyrinth of sorrow where hope felt like a distant ember, flickering and fragile.

A tremor laced my breath as a whimper escaped, barely more than a whisper: "Just one, Lord." The words trembled in the silence; a plea wrapped in desperation. But the weight of longing crushed my restraint, and the quiet murmur swelled into sobs, raw and unshackled. Tears traced burning paths down my dirty little face as my cry fractured the midnight stillness, rising with the urgency of a heart laid bare.

"Just one, Lord!"

The darkness didn't answer, but somewhere, beyond sight, beyond certainty, I hoped Jesus was listening.

I wasn't yearning for an idealized hero—a knight on a white horse. No, I simply prayed for someone who could *see* me, someone who could understand my pain. But that night, no one came.

For years, I suffered alone, pleading and begging for help— yet no one heard the cries of the child within me. It wasn't until adulthood that someone finally recognized what I'd never been able to say out loud: a wordless, urgent cry for rescue. You see, that is who I was in my brokenness—a shattered, abused child. My mind longed for salvation, for someone—*anyone*—to step in, but my body had become hardened by the beatings. Would anyone see the dying child within? With each unanswered plea, my hope withered. And tragically... no one was brave enough to acknowledge the truth, step in, or respond to my cries for help.

Too often, we turn a blind eye to the suffering that unfolds in the shadows—caught between uncertainty and fear—unsure of how to intervene, paralyzed by the weight of responsibility. We silence the quiet voice within us that whispers, *"Something isn't right."* We hesitate—convincing ourselves that someone else will step in, that it isn't our battle to fight, that looking away is easier than facing the truth.

Years later, some found the courage to admit what their hearts already knew—that they sensed something was wrong, that they felt the unease, but fear held them captive, *fear* of being wrong, *fear* of meddling, and *fear* of what it might cost to take action. And yet, there are others—those who avert their eyes when I pass, burdened by guilt they refuse to name. They carry the weight of their silence, their inaction, their refusal to see what was always there. But instead of facing that truth, they turn to condemnation—for dismissal, for avoidance, even for their persecution. Not because I deserve it, but because it's easier to villainize me than to reckon with their own regret. But truth doesn't bend beneath the pressure of denial. It doesn't disappear in avoidance. And whether they choose to acknowledge it or not, it remains—a quiet, unyielding testament to what was, to what should have been, and to what must never happen again.

Amid the silence, when the weight of loneliness threatened to consume me, *one* individual reached out. And that single act

of compassion—small in gesture but immeasurable in impact—
became the lifeline that pulled me from the shadows, giving me
the strength to write this book today.

My first book peeled back the layers of my childhood,
exposing the raw wounds, the pain, the battles fought in secret.
But I knew there was more. My story wasn't just about
survival—it was about redemption, transformation, and stepping
forward as a voice—not just for myself, but for others still
waiting to be heard.

Now, I speak not out of bitterness, but out of *purpose*. I cry
out as a warning bell, pleading for someone—*anyone*—to hear
the call. To be the one who sees, who reaches, who refuses to
turn away. Because somewhere, a voice still calls from the
darkness, trembling yet hopeful—"Just one."

Can you hear it? The quiet, pleading voices that too often
fade into the background—swallowed by indifference, drowned
in silence? Will you answer? Or will their cries, once again, fall
upon deaf ears? The time for waiting is over. The time for
assuming it's someone else's responsibility has passed. *Now* is
the time to rise. It's time to step beyond the comfort of our
churches, beyond the safety of familiarity, and reach the
countless hurting souls—children and adults alike—who are
longing, aching, pleading to be heard. Their voices aren't scarce.
Their cries aren't few. The problem isn't their numbers—the true
issue lies in our unwillingness to listen, in our hesitation to act,
in the fear that whispers, *"What if I'm not enough?"*

217

Perhaps we feel inadequate. Perhaps doubt convinces us that we are unprepared, unqualified, incapable of making a difference. But hear this: Our ability to help doesn't come from education, our social status or wealth. It comes from obedience. It comes from surrender.

We are called. We are equipped. And the only requirement—the only thing He asks of us—is a willing heart. A heart that cries out, "Lord, use me."

So, will you step forward, unshaken and resolute? Will you *be the one*—a light in the shadows, an answer to the plea etched in trembling voices? Or will the cries, desperate and fading, slip once more into the abyss of silence, swallowed by indifference, lost to the void of unanswered prayers? The moment stands before you. The choice is yours.

God doesn't just mend what's broken—*He Restores.* He takes the shattered pieces and weaves them into something stronger, something purposeful. And in His restoration, He doesn't call us to simply receive healing—He calls us to extend it. To be the hand that reaches into the darkness. To be the voice that speaks life into the weary. To be the living testimony that survival isn't the end of the story—*redemption is.*

Someone reached out to me when I was lost in the depths of desolation—a single act of compassion became the bridge between despair and hope. And now, it's my turn. My time to reach back, to step into the trenches, to minister to those who are still waiting—*waiting* to be seen, *waiting* to be heard, *waiting* for someone to fight for them. I've walked through the fire. I've been refined, tested, and shaped by the flames. And I've emerged whole—whole enough to hear the voices calling, whole enough to reach into the suffering, whole enough to carry the message of healing to those who believe they are too broken to be restored. Because no one is beyond redemption. And I will spend every day ensuring that they know it.

There have been moments when I have stood in stunned silence—shaken to my core by words spoken from the very place that should embody grace: the Church. The weight of condemnation, sharp and unrelenting, has echoed through its halls, turning sacred spaces into arenas of judgment. Too often, people are not seen in the fullness of their humanity but are instead reduced to labels—heavy chains that bind them, their struggles plastered over their identities like scars that refuse to heal.

Angry, bitter, liar, murderer, narcissist, homosexual, drunkard, drug dealer, adulterer—each name a brand, seared into the skin, pressing deeper with every whisper, every cold stare, every sermon that wields righteousness like a weapon. And the list goes on, stretching endlessly, a litany of condemnation that crushes the soul beneath the weight of supposed holiness. But is this our calling? Is this truly the heart of Christ?

Didn't He kneel in the dust, lifting the face of the woman accused? Didn't He dine with the tax collector, touch the leper, restore the dignity of the forgotten? Should we, in our flawed humanity, proclaim judgment over another's brokenness—or should we ask the deeper question—*why?*

Why does anger linger? Why does bitterness take root? Why does the liar feel the need to deceive... the drunk to escape... the adulterer to search for something missing? Perhaps the answer isn't in the condemnation—but in the invitation—to listen, to understand, to extend the kind of love that doesn't erase the past—but dares to redeem it. Maybe grace was never meant to be selective but extravagant, a flood instead of a trickle. Perhaps it's not our place to cast stones, but to open doors.

Pain is never random; it doesn't erupt without cause. It's forged in the fire of rejection, etched into the soul by loss, betrayal, loneliness—silent wounds that the world fails to see. Pain burrows deep, shaping the way a person moves, speaks, reacts, until suffering is no longer just an experience, but an identity worn like armor. And if God has opened our eyes to this ache—if He has pressed on our hearts the weight of another's sorrow—then He has entrusted us with a sacred duty.

We aren't called to stand at a distance, cool and detached, measuring another's worth through the lens of past mistakes. We aren't sent to cast verdicts like stones, to let judgment fall where mercy should reign. We are called to reach—to lift the weary from their depths, to press love into the cracks of a broken spirit, to embrace without condition, to look past the outburst, the bitterness, the rebellion, and see the wounded child beneath—aching, searching, desperate for relief. To refuse to ignore their cries, to kneel in the dust beside them, whispering hope into the darkness. Because Christ didn't come to condemn—He came to heal. And if we claim to follow in His footsteps, then we must move as He does—with hands open, arms outstretched, love pouring forth in reckless, unreserved abundance.

So put down the stones and let judgment fall away. Extend grace like a flood, not a trickle, because behind every hardened heart is a soul still longing to be seen.

I must confess—my journey hasn't been shaped by a single voice, nor guided by just one hand. It's been an orchestra of hearts, a symphony of souls answering God's call, weaving their stories into mine. Some have left footprints so deep they'll never fade—their impact carved into the very foundation of my being. Others faltered, never truly grasping their worth—drifting like echoes lost in the wind. Some lost themselves along the way, their light dimmed by the weight of the world, while others stood firm, refining me, as iron sharpens iron.

If I dared to name each person who has touched my life, these pages would stretch beyond measure—spilling over with moments of grace and quiet revelations. But hear me: My heart overflows with gratitude. Every soul God has placed in my path has, in some way, heard the silent cry within. Each one—knowingly or unknowingly—answered the call to walk alongside me, to shape, to challenge, and to help me heal.

And yet, I don't contradict myself when I say: Be the one. Yes, God will send others. Yes, you may not always be the final

221

hand that ushers someone into freedom. But make no mistake—your reach matters. You don't own the souls you minister to; you are simply the willing vessel. We don't initiate the call or dictate the outcome—we simply yield to His Spirit and trust Him to work *through* us.

Because it only takes one. One voice to hear the cry... One heart to reach out... One hand to ignite transformation... Though our ministries differ, though our methods may vary, together, *we become the church.* And the church—when it moves in unity, when it walks in grace—*is* the answer.

Can we truly make an impact? Can we cast aside hesitation, silence the whisper of fear, and step boldly into the calling laid before us? Or will we remain insulated—cocooned in the familiar, safely detached, watching the world from behind the veil of our own comfort? The hour is urgent, the need—undeniable. Souls are crying out, time slipping through our fingers like grains of sand.

Whether you've walked through fire, stood firm in truth, or are just beginning the journey to healing—it's time. The weight of this moment is no accident. You didn't pick up this book by chance. Hear the voice that calls you now—Jesus asks, "Wilt thou be made whole?"

Healing, ministry, the very essence of life itself—it all begins with one whispered plea: *"Lord, let me hear the cries around me. Let me see through Your eyes."*

But take heed—once you speak these words, the world will never look the same. Your vision will sharpen; what once seemed like anger, bitterness, rebellion will dissolve before your eyes. No longer will defiance stand before you like an unyielding wall—its edges will soften; its barriers will fade. In its place, you will see trembling souls, weary and worn, their strength eroded beneath the suffocating weight of their sorrow. Their silent cries will no longer be masked by hardened exteriors; their unseen hands, outstretched in desperation, will reach for solace, for rescue—for anything that might lift them from the abyss of their pain.

Lord Jesus, shift our perspective. Break through the barriers of misunderstanding. Teach us to see that pain erects walls—not choice, not intent. No soul is born yearning for callousness; no heart begins its journey craving to grow cold. Beneath the layers of brokenness, beyond the wounds and defenses, there is a silent plea—a longing for someone to be the answer, to stand in the gap, to embody love in its purest form.

Again, I say: Be the church. Not in name alone, but in action, in sacrifice, in love that pierces through the darkness and transforms the world—one soul at a time.

Perhaps it's *you* who is silently crying out, your soul aching beneath the weight of unspoken fears. Don't let hesitation bind you, nor let the shadows of uncertainty keep you from the light. Reach and pray, ask Jesus for guidance, for an open door—and when He places it before you, don't refuse it. Step forward in faith and walk through.

I understand the trembling uncertainty, the restless war between longing and fear. I know the weight of that first step. I will never forget the moment I entered that humble little Country Pentecostal Church—my heart pounding like a battle drum against my ribs. The raw presence of the Spirit engulfed me, so powerful, so overwhelming—I ran. Fear whispered that I was unworthy, that surrender would change everything—and it did. Days passed, but the longing only deepened. I couldn't escape it; something greater was calling, something beyond my understanding. When I returned, the floodgates opened. What once felt unreachable suddenly became an embrace—a love so boundless, so undeniable, that every fear crumbled beneath its weight.

If Jesus is guiding your path, then beyond your fear lies the fulfillment your soul has longed for. *Trust—every step is worth it.* And when the time comes—when His voice calls you to step forward in ministry, to become the hands that reach, the voice that speaks life into broken places—*do not hesitate.*

There's no greater privilege than to be the one who answers, to step beyond self and into divine purpose. To bring light into the wilderness, to stand in the gap, to embody the call of God. *This is your moment.* Go.

Through the years, God has gifted me the sacred privilege of ministering—of walking beside others in their healing, witnessing the quiet miracles of restoration. Among those moments, one remains etched upon my heart with an eternal imprint: the healing of my bond with my twin sister—my dearest friend, the reflection of my own soul. I've watched God gather the shattered fragments of her heart, gently piecing them back together with a love only He can give. Her wounds ran deep, her struggles pressed heavy upon her spirit. And yet, the first time I reached for her, something undeniable stirred within me—a recognition, a revelation. I knew her pain because I had walked it. I carried the same weight, bore the same scars.

For years, we drifted—two vessels caught in opposing tides, carried by currents we couldn't control. But then... God moved. The waters shifted, and He drifted us back into alignment, weaving our journeys together once more. I understood her fears—because they were mine. I saw her battles—because I had fought them. Today, I rejoice in the radiance of her transformation—in the beauty of the soul God is shaping within her. And as I stand in awe, I see more than just my sister. I see a warrior of God rising, strengthened by grace, emboldened by faith, walking boldly into the divine purpose He has prepared for her.

There was a time when I believed I had failed—when doubt whispered that my efforts had been in vain, that my prayers had gone unanswered. But as I watched healing take root, something deeper stirred within me—wholeness was unfolding, not just for her, but within us *both*. A divine weaving of restoration, threading through the fabric of our lives. The next time God opened a door, I stepped through with renewed strength—no longer leaning on my own understanding but drawing my direction... my very breath... from Him. In the beginning, I had rushed ahead, eager for her transformation to come like a sudden flood. But God, in His infinite wisdom, revealed a truth I had yet to grasp: *Healing is not a race—it's a journey.* She had to walk her path at her own pace, just as I had walked mine. And in that revelation, *I found peace.*

Over the years, I have watched her walk through pain—her hands outstretched even as she herself was still healing. Some will never understand her. Because they never took the time—to listen, to see, to grasp the depth of her story. They never saw her the way God sees her. But despite the rejection... despite the persecution... she refuses to yield. She presses forward—a warrior in motion, embracing her personal journey toward wholeness with unshaken resolve. And through it all, God has allowed us to minister *together*—to speak with unguarded honesty, to share our battles, to celebrate our victories, to reach for those who tread the same weary paths. I only wish my sister could fully see the extraordinary woman of God she is. *I see her*—not just in the triumphs, but in the struggles, in the quiet battles waged behind closed doors, in the moments where pain threatens to steal her strength.

She doesn't need to shape herself to fit the world's expectations or measure her worth against anyone else. She is *enough*. She is already *remarkable*. Her strength is *undeniable*. She has endured so very much—yet she stands—unwavering, resilient—a living testament to faith, perseverance, and the refining power of grace. She amazes me *every day.* She is an overcomer, a fighter, a victor, and I admire her deeply for all that she is.

I pray she never doubts how cherished she is, how deeply we love her, how much her presence is valued. May she always know that she is seen—that she is held in the highest regard by those who walk this journey beside her.

I'm profoundly grateful that God, in His mercy, granted me the precious gift of restoration also with my mother—the chance to mend what had once been broken, to reclaim love that had long been kept at bay. For years, anger had built a fortress between us, walls of hurt and misunderstanding that barred connection, casting shadows over what should have been light.

But now, I understand the weight of time, the devotion of relationship, the irreplaceable treasure of each moment. My mother was a gift—a reflection of grace, and I was honored to call her mother. The mother my heart had longed for... I found in the end. In her embrace, I felt love—true, unshakable love—and in that moment, revelation swept through like a rushing wind: *She had struggled too.* She had carried burdens unseen, wrestled with wounds long hidden beneath the surface. For so long, I'd only seen my pain, but now, I saw hers. She was fighting battles I'd never fully understood. And it was my honor to walk beside her in truth—to witness her journey unfold in divine grace. Among my life's greatest joys was the moment I watched her surrender—her baptism in Jesus' name, the infilling of the Holy Ghost, the radiant light that overtook her just months before she stepped into eternity: *Restoration came in time.*

And when that final hour arrived, I was there. I was beside her when she took her last breath, knowing—without doubt— that healing had come. That God had redeemed what was lost. That love had triumphed over everything that once stood in its way. If there is one lesson I've learned, it is this: *Time is fleeting.* Don't wait. Don't let fear or hesitation steal what can still be made whole. Don't assume there will be another opportunity— there may not be. Reach for your family now, while you can. Believe—and let God do the rest. So often, we grow frustrated with others—disappointed, wounded—because they do not meet our expectations. We seek perfection, forgetting that we ourselves are far from flawless. But the truth? There is only One who is perfect, and His name is Jesus. If we do not acknowledge our frailties, we will forever be ensnared in the trap of judgment—disillusioned by the imperfections of those around us, and blind to the grace we so desperately need ourselves.

Mistakes will come. The enemy will seize them—twisting them into weapons, whispering condemnation into the depths of our soul. He is the master deceiver, the father of lies, and yet— how often do we listen? How often do we shrink beneath the weight of his accusations, retreating into silence... into despair? But hear me: *Stop listening.* Shut out the voice that tells you redemption is impossible. Cast off the chains of doubt and turn to Jesus.

It wasn't until I embraced this truth that healing finally began within my family. I saw them for who they truly were—not villains, not obstacles, but souls—wounded, weary, longing to be understood. Their anger... their frustration... their missteps were the echoes of their own battles. And just as I had suffered, so had they. Just as I had grieved, so had they. The mercy of Jesus reshaped my vision—softening the calluses of my heart. And in His light, I saw them as He did: not as enemies, but as kindred souls in need of grace.

I often wonder how different my life would have been if someone had reached for me sooner? Would it have changed the course of my journey? Or did the fire of adversity forge the hunger within me—the unrelenting thirst that can't be quenched, except through ministry? I believe the latter. There is something within me—burning, aching—a cry that refuses to be silenced. A longing to reach the world. But I know I can't do it alone. That's why I turn to you.

You are here. You cared enough to open this book, to hear these words. Somewhere in your life, there is someone struggling—someone crying out, "Does anyone care?" Perhaps they are the thorn in your side—the one whose anger bewilders you, whose bitterness repels you. Or maybe they are silent souls—carrying wounds too deep to voice. But you're not here to remain unchanged. You are *called*—to reach, to love, to heal.

Through the years, I've witnessed countless journeys unfolding on the path to restoration. Some pressed forward and found wholeness. Others hesitated—lingering in brokenness, settling for less than what God intended. My heart longs to cry out, *"Keep going! Do not stop now!"* But I've learned a sobering truth: Wholeness is unattainable unless they cry out to *Jesus*. He alone is the missing piece—the cornerstone of restoration. Without Him, wholeness remains a distant dream.

But hear me: Jesus is not merely a refuge in desperation. He isn't an ATM—dispensing blessings upon demand. He is the *Lover of your soul*, the One who desires your *whole* heart—not fleeting devotion, not surface faith, but surrender. Life is a journey—a storm of highs and lows, triumphs and sorrows. What separates stagnation from transformation is *Perspective*. Until we recognize that Jesus is the key, we will remain lost. Can you hear Him? Can you see Him? He is calling still: *"Wilt thou be made whole?"* The choice is yours.

Understand this: *Imperfection isn't failure.* It's often the very thing that shapes us, strengthens us, and propels us toward transformation—in the right hands. And those hands belong to Jesus. Look into His Word, and you will see: every miracle, every act of divine intervention was poured out upon those who had reached the end of themselves, those who had lost hope. And yet—*Jesus stepped in.* In Him, there is hope eternal.

To be whole doesn't mean to be flawless. It means to be sustained by a hope that can't be shaken—to awaken each morning knowing that Jesus will provide the strength for the journey ahead.

Now that you have glimpsed a part of my journey—one carved through the fires of pain and victory—don't waste another moment yearning for change. *Step forward in Jesus.* Be the change. Open your heart to the people He places in your path. Walk boldly into the ministry to which He is calling you. Each of us bears a purpose, each of us carries a calling. The question is—*will you allow Jesus to use you?*

Today is a new beginning. It starts here. It starts now. I want you to experience the wholeness Jesus has prepared for you. Whether this is your first attempt at restoration, whether you are saint or sinner, abuser or abused—I pray that every wound, every regret, every ounce of brokenness begins to heal in Jesus' Name. I pray that as you pursue wholeness, you encounter the *Peace Speaker*—the One who knows you by name. That He directs your every step, that He surrounds you with people who will walk beside you in faith. I pray He blesses you with strength, endurance, and determination—that this time, there will be no turning back, no giving up. I pray that the enemy's voice is silenced, that you hear only the voice of God. And above all—I pray that you find the courage to share your testimony. That the world may see that wholeness is possible in Him.

Remember: *"The only impossible journey is the one you never begin."* Your journey starts with trusting God, with taking that *first* step. Trust me—you will never regret living for Him. Godspeed, my friend, as you embark on your *"Journey to Wholeness"*—or extend your hand to guide another.

Thirteen: Awakened

Rising Into Divine Fulfillment

*I*t's often said that the number thirteen carries an air of misfortune; yet today, it stands as a beacon of divine progression—a pivotal moment in the unfolding of God's call. So often, we view struggles and hardships as unwelcome intrusions—shadows of bad luck looming over our lives. But when we step back, when we reflect, a deeper truth emerges: God is faithful, steadfast, and true. Every trial, every storm-tossed night, every valley of uncertainty was never a setback, but a steppingstone. Each difficulty crafted a purpose—shaping a ministry not by accident, but by design. God's design. And now, as I gaze upon the tapestry He has so beautifully woven, I stand in awe. It is a masterpiece far beyond what I could have envisioned—a testament to His unfailing grace and the extraordinary artistry of His will.

Every trial, every sleepless night, every tear-stained prayer was never a curse, but a chapter in a greater narrative—a story of refinement, preparation, and divine purpose. A ministry is not birthed in the comforts of ease, nor shaped in the absence of struggle. It's forged in the crucible of adversity, tempered by fire, and sculpted by His sovereign hand to fulfill a calling far beyond our imagination.

We never envisioned standing where we are today. Each hardship, each moment of anguish, became more than just a memory—they became the foundation stones of something greater. And though the wounds of the past still whisper their presence, we rise—not in defeat, but in the strength that only surrender can bring. Because the true power of achievement isn't found in the struggle itself, but in the transformation it ignites. It's through the breaking that we are remade, through the refining that we are strengthened—until what was once pain now breathes life, hope, and healing into countless hearts.

For years, I bore the scars of battle—wounds not only of the flesh, but of the soul. The weight was relentless, pressing upon my spirit—mental anguish, physical pain, sexual abuse, the silent echoes of the past, the turmoil of uncertainty. These wounds whispered lies, threatening to define me, to chain me to a history I could not rewrite. And yet, amid the quiet stirring of my heart, a question emerged: *Could my past be more than a burden?* Could the shattered fragments of my journey be woven into something beautiful, something purposeful? Perhaps a ministry, perhaps counseling, I questioned. A place where brokenness could be transformed into healing.

I watched my husband walk unwaveringly in his calling—Children's Evangelism inscribed upon his spirit with certainty; his path anchored in clarity. There was never a doubt that he would flourish. But I doubted myself. How could I contribute meaningfully when my own path felt undefined, when I felt lost in comparison? Where did I belong? Was I merely a support, destined to linger in the shadows, holding up another's purpose while my own remained hidden? The question gnawed at my soul.

Silently, I feared that I was more of a hindrance than a help. I longed to feel the fire of certainty that burned so brightly within him. But my heart? My heart remained unlit—untouched by the same conviction. At least, that's what I thought.

In the early years, I found solace in the background—content to serve, as long as I remained unseen. I crafted my comfort zone carefully, convinced that my role was behind the scenes, never at the forefront. What I didn't realize was that God was weaving something grander—something unexpected, something I never saw coming. The ministry began to evolve—stretching beyond the limits I had quietly placed around it, growing in ways I never imagined. Then came the moments that forced me out of my self-imposed sanctuary. The moments that pulled me forward, urging me to step into the unknown. I resisted—how could I not? Fear whispered its doubts; insecurity held me captive. And yet, through the chaos of my hesitation, God's voice broke through—steady, sure, and unmistakable: *"Trust Me."*

And so, with trembling faith... I did. With every act of surrender, something extraordinary began to unfold. My carefully guarded walls gave way, my comfort zone stretched, and the fractures of my heart mended beneath the tender hands of grace. What had once felt like mere obedience became something far greater—an ignition, a Holy fire kindled within me, burning with an unshakable love for souls, for the altar, for the boundless and unfathomable power of God's presence.

I'd been blessed time and again, but now, the miracles were no longer distant—they surrounded me, wrapped themselves around my spirit, moving not only within me but all around me.

There is something breathtakingly sacred about witnessing transformation—about watching chains shatter, burdens lift, and lives awaken. To stand in the presence of the miraculous is to feel Heaven brush against earth, to glimpse the hand of God moving in ways beyond comprehension. And what I once resisted, became my greatest joy.

One truth resonates deeply: the Body of Christ is a symphony of many parts—each essential, each irreplaceable. No role is lesser, no calling insignificant. And within this divine tapestry, I have discovered immeasurable joy in a gift I once overlooked: the simple yet profound ministry of laughter. What I once regarded as frivolous and fearful, I now see as a bridge, a balm—a healer, it was a means of opening doors that might have otherwise remained closed. Laughter softens hearts, dissolves barriers, and breathes light into spaces weighed down by sorrow.

And to my astonishment, I've fallen in love with Children's Ministry—a place I never imagined would become my home, my passion. It hasn't only exceeded my every expectation—it has shattered the limits of what I once believed possible. In the wide-eyed wonder of a child, in the purity of their faith, I've witnessed transformation—not just in them, but in myself. What I once hesitated to embrace has become the very thing that fuels my spirit.

One of the greatest challenges in the church today is the tendency to confine ministries within rigid compartments—to see them as singular functions rather than living, breathing extensions of God's limitless reach. Children's Ministry, in particular, is often viewed as serving only the young—its impact seemingly limited to little hands and learning hearts. But this perception misses the divine reality: Its influence doesn't end with childhood. It ripples outward—shaping families, strengthening communities, igniting revival and enriching the body of Christ as a whole.

God never intended His calling to be bound by human definitions. His reach is boundless, His love unwavering. His invitation—*for whosoever will.*

This revelation didn't come easily. My husband and I embarked upon this journey believing we were building a specialized ministry—something structured, something confined. But God was painting something far greater than we imagined: a masterpiece woven with eternal threads, rich with purpose, flowing with grace, and reaching far beyond what we could see. This was never about a single generation or a singular mission. It's always been about lives being touched at every stage, hearts being transformed across every season.

Where my husband flourished, I found my place of support. Where I thrived, he stood beside me. And together—step by step—we became a living testimony of divine partnership, not shaped by human expectation, but by the sovereign hand of God.

Today, our greatest joy isn't found in the label of *Children's Ministry*. The truth is, we are a vital, thriving part of the greater Church body. Our mission doesn't exist in isolation—it reaches, it uplifts, it restores. It moves beyond generations, beyond titles, beyond expectations, speaking to the hearts of many.

And above all, we remain unwavering in our commitment: that every soul—young or old, searching or steadfast—would encounter the transformative, healing, all-consuming love of God. This isn't just what we do; *It's who we are.*

This is our ministry—This is our purpose—This is our joy.

Through every trial, every challenge, and every moment of uncertainty, God has revealed an undeniable truth: none of it was without purpose. Every hardship was a steppingstone, every struggle a refinement—shaping our strength, our direction and our anointing.

What once felt like obstacles were, in fact, the very foundation stones upon which He was building something far greater than we could have imagined.

God's Handywork Inc. was not born from human ambition, nor crafted by our own wisdom—it was established by His divine hand, woven together with the strengths and weaknesses of those involved, perfectly aligned with His will. Many mistakenly believe it's *our* ministry—something we built, something we control. But through experience, through revelation, we have come to understand the truth: it is, and always has been, and always will be—His ministry. His vision. His masterpiece. We are simply the vessels—entrusted to carry out what He has already designed.

This is where your journey begins, dear reader. Whether you have already found healing, are searching for it, or feel compelled to be a part of another's restoration, the path forward calls for reflection. True transformation doesn't happen in isolation—it is woven through the tapestry of time, stitched together with the threads of past victories and wounds.

Before we can step fully into God's purpose, we must first turn our gaze backward—not to be held captive by what has been, but to recognize His fingerprints upon every step, every struggle, every breakthrough.

Healing was never meant to be our final destination. It is only the beginning—a gateway leading to something far greater, a sacred wholeness where restoration deepens and reveals new purpose. For in wholeness, we don't merely mend; we are remade. We don't simply survive; we are transformed. This is the essence of walking with God—not pausing at the place of healing but pressing forward into a life fully aligned with His divine will.

And in this wholeness, *nothing* is wasted. Every tear, every trial, every moment of uncertainty—is reshaped, redeemed, and woven into a masterpiece beyond human comprehension. The wounds that once threatened to destroy us become testimonies of His unfailing grace. The burdens that once weighed us down now become bridges—leading others to the same restoration we found. We were never meant to carry our redemption in silence. We are called to shine, to radiate, to become luminous beacons in a weary world—reflections of the love that healed us, the grace that sustained us, and the wholeness that transformed us. And so, the journey begins. Not just toward healing, but toward *divine fullness*. Not just to be restored... but to become vessels of His love, instruments of His purpose, bearers of His eternal light.

Before I continue, allow me to impart one more truth—one that speaks to the sacred task of supporting the wounded, whether emotionally or spiritually. It's much like tending to an injured creature, trembling and uncertain. Often, they do not recognize the kindness extended to them, nor do they comprehend the hand that reaches out in compassion. Their pain erects walls—fortresses built from mistrust, shaped by the weight of past wounds, guarded by the fear of being hurt again.

These barriers, though invisible, are impenetrable to anything less than unwavering patience and relentless grace. And yes, it can be disheartening... when your earnest attempts to offer compassion are met with hesitation, doubt, or even rejection. But in these moments, when rejection stings and hopes seem dim, remember this: *Grace was once extended to you, too.* And love—especially when it's unfamiliar—isn't always immediately embraced.

Some souls, upon encountering *genuine* love for the first time, cling to it with a desperate intensity—not out of weakness, but out of a longing for assurance, proof that it will not fade like so many fragile hopes before it. They hold on tightly, searching for certainty, pleading for stability, something real; speak to that longing, offer the steady presence of unshaken compassion.

Be the lighthouse in their storm—the fixed beacon that refuses to dim, the light that slices through the fog of fear and doubt. Assure them: Your presence is not temporary; your care isn't conditional, that healing is not merely a distant dream—it's a promise within reach. And when, at last, their guarded hearts exhale...when their grip loosens and trust begins to bloom—believe this: the love you offered will become their light. A flame carried forward, a fire that leads others into the fullness of restoration.

Though they may find a measure of peace in their present state, believing it to be a sanctuary, a refuge from the burdens they have carried, gently encourage them to take a bold step forward—to press beyond survival into the fullness of faith, to trust in the limitless abundance of God. Their present comfort, however safe it may seem, is not their final dwelling place; it is but a resting point on the journey toward wholeness.

Remind them: What you offer—however sincere and meaningful—is but a glimpse of the vast love and restoration found in Him. Your words, your presence, your compassion—all of it is but a reflection, a mere whisper of the infinite healing that awaits them in His embrace. For there is so much more—a depth of grace beyond imagination, a wholeness so complete that it doesn't simply mend wounds but reshapes them, weaving them into the fabric of *new purpose*. Encourage them to trust, to step forward, to surrender—not just to healing... but to *transformation*. And in that surrender, they will find what their heart has truly been searching for—not just refuge, but renewal.

To the one who struggles to heal—you have absorbed the wisdom above but hear this clearly: Awareness alone does not grant permission to linger in stagnation. Healing is not passive; it's a journey that demands movement, for it requires courage rather than mere acknowledgment. What I'm about to share may feel uncomfortable, but I wish someone had loved me enough to say it: *Sometimes, true healing begins not in comfort, but in confrontation.* Sometimes, the most transformative breakthroughs come not in gentle reassurance but through the sharp, unmistakable clarity of truth—even when it stings.

The one walking beside you—the one offering their unwavering presence and pouring out their strength—is not merely a witness to your pain. They are *bearing it with you*, carrying what they can so that you might begin to lay down the weight. And yet, resistance—though human, though understandable—can become an anchor, pulling not only you but them into the depths of uncertainty. They see you. They perceive the battle behind your silence, the wounds you have yet to name. And they know that no matter how steadfast their love, it's but a pale reflection of the love God longs to pour into you—a love that is infinite, relentless, and all-consuming.

But understand this—they were not placed in your life to be your god, but to be His hands and feet, a vessel of mercy, to guide you toward the only true source of healing. Don't allow fear to trap you in hesitation. Don't let comfort deceive you into complacency.

Embrace their presence. Treasure their effort. And most importantly, honor their sacrifice with growth. Let their encouragement challenge you, stretch you, and propel you toward the fullness of the restoration waiting in God. Healing was never meant to be merely received; it was meant to be lived.

Understand this: God, in His boundless wisdom, places many souls along your journey—not just one. Each is there to illuminate your path through life's trials. Each carries a distinct voice, a perspective woven with divine purpose, offering you layers of insight that enrich your healing and transformation. No encounter is random; no moment is wasted. Every presence in your life is a thread in the grand tapestry of your growth— carefully stitched by His loving hand. Be open to the guidance He provides, for within each connection lies the whisper of His divine orchestration.

Just as the earth moves through its rhythmic seasons, so does the unfolding of your restoration. Some seasons beckon stillness—inviting reflection and quiet renewal. Others call for pruning—an unyielding stripping away of what no longer serves you, clearing the soil for new life to flourish. And then, the moments of full bloom arrives—radiant, abundant, a living testimony to resilience and grace.

Embrace the nurturing hands of the Master Gardener, for His care is intentional and transformative. Every touch, every shift, every gentle replanting is by design. The wind may press against you, the soil may feel unfamiliar—but growth was never meant to be comfortable. It's meant to refine, shape, and mold you into all you are created to be. Trust the hands that cultivate your purpose, and in time, you will rise in the fullness of His restoration—blossoming, unshaken, and whole.

Healing and transformation are not solitary pursuits; they are sacred journeys woven through connection, nourished by the love and wisdom of those God has placed along your path. Just as a flower can't flourish without the touch of pollination, neither can the soul thrive in isolation. Open your heart to the hands that uplift, to the voices that speak life, to the presence of those who remind you of His unwavering grace. These relationships are no mere coincidence—they are divine appointments, vessels of His purpose, designed to fortify your faith, strengthen your spirit, and illuminate your calling.

Above all, surrender. Trust that even in the moments when change feels unsettling, when the road ahead is blurred by uncertainty, God is leading with a steady and sovereign hand. You were never meant to carry this journey alone. Embrace the beauty of being shaped, nurtured, and cultivated through life's ever-changing seasons—knowing that each transition, each challenge, each act of faith leads you closer to the fullness of His divine plan.

Now, you stand at the crossroads of your story—a sacred threshold where the past must finally release its grip, where burdens, long carried, must fall away like sand slipping through your fingers, dissolving into the tide. These weights have clung to you like relentless shadows, veiling the light, stifling growth, burying possibility beneath their suffocating pressure. And where healing should have bloomed, bitterness has crept in—twisting through wounds like thorned vines, entwining itself around your scars, refusing to release its grip.

But *release* is the doorway to transformation—the divine turning point where grace breathes into the hollow spaces of your soul, where the fractures of your past surrender to the radiant touch of restoration. It's here, at the edge of renewal, that light pierces the darkness—gentle yet unyielding—spilling across the landscape of your heart like the first blush of dawn awakening the earth.

This is the moment, the unspoken invitation to step forward, to relinquish the weight that was never meant to be carried. For though the past may have shaped you, it doesn't hold the authority to define you. What lies ahead is untouched, unmarred, waiting—bathed in possibility, overflowing with promise. Breathe deeply and allow His grace to restore you. Now, step boldly into the dawn of what has always been destined for you.

"See to it that no one falls short of the grace of God and that no bitter root grows up to cause trouble and defile many."
—*Hebrews 12:15 NIV*

Bitterness is an insidious thief—quiet, cunning, creeping through the corridors of the heart, unraveling the delicate tapestry of healing that God so patiently weaves. It doesn't storm in as an obvious invader but moves in secrecy, like a whisper threading its way through wounded places; a seed buried deep in soil tinged with disappointment, betrayal, and the shattered remnants of unfulfilled dreams. At first, it seems harmless, scarcely noticeable—a fleeting thought, a lingering sting. But left unchallenged, it germinates, its roots burrowing into the depths of the soul, twisting into resentment and entwining itself with every cherished belief. It distorts vision, turning light into shadow, hope into cynicism, faith into doubt. Poison seeps into the veins of relationships, eroding trust, silencing joy, and breeding division where harmony once flourished.

Like invasive weeds choking life from a once-thriving garden, bitterness resists containment. It spreads quietly but persistently—creeping from one wounded heart to the next, tainting interactions, suffocating grace, and dimming the radiance of God's restoration. In its wake, it leaves a landscape barren—once lush with love, now desolate with sorrow. Yet, even in the grip of its suffocating hold, redemption is never beyond reach. For where bitterness thrives, grace can uproot. Where shadows fall, light can break through. The cycle is broken in surrender—in offering every wound to the hands of the Divine. And in that surrender, beauty—once lost—is restored anew.

God calls us beyond the suffocating grip of bitterness. He beckons us into the boundless expanse of freedom—where hearts are unburdened and souls are set free. Forgiveness isn't a concession of defeat or a dismissal of injustice; it's a sacred exchange, a divine transaction in which the weight of past wounds is surrendered, and grace rushes in like a river—cleansing the soil where pain once took root.

Even Christ—suspended between heaven and earth, scarred by betrayal, broken by cruelty—poured out mercy in His agony. His love didn't falter beneath the crushing blow of rejection, nor did His compassion wane beneath the burden of suffering. If His grace could rise above the shadows of condemnation, then

surely, by His power, ours can transcend the wounds of
yesterday.

The key to dismantling bitterness is *surrender*—not simply
loosening our grip on past offenses but entrusting them into the
hands of the One who redeems all things. Instead of rehearsing
our sorrows like a well-worn melody, we invite Jesus to
compose a new song within us—one of restoration and renewal.
Instead of clinging to resentment, we ask for the courage to
extend grace—grace that defies every justification for holding on
to hurt. When bitterness whispers its lies, insisting that pain is
our only protection, we stand in Holy defiance, proclaiming that
mercy reigns higher, love stands unshaken, and healing is
already unfolding beneath the touch of the Almighty.

So today, let us rise in the radiance of His peace. Let joy
swell within us like a triumphant anthem, silencing every echo of
resentment. May grace be our testimony—our banner unfurled in
victory. Let love be our dwelling place—steadfast, unyielding
and true. His love is greater—greater than every wound, every
sorrow, every injustice. His love remains—immovable and
infinite—and in Him, we are truly free.

We have arrived at the threshold of the most sacred—and
most difficult—step in your journey: *Forgiveness.* To forgive
isn't to diminish the gravity of the wounds inflicted upon you,
nor to erase the echoes of suffering that have shaped you. It's the
defiant act of reclaiming your life—the bold refusal to allow
your past to dictate your future. Forgiveness isn't weakness, but

an unyielding strength that transcends bitterness, a fire that refuses to be extinguished by the weight of pain.

You stand at the precipice of transformation, staring into the abyss of memory—not with fear, but with the wisdom of a soul that has endured... that has fought... and has risen. And here, in this moment, you choose not to be shackled by resentment, not to be bound by rage; but to rise and declare, with unwavering authority:

"You will no longer define me. You will no longer control me. You will no longer have power over me."

And just like that, the chains that once strangled your spirit begin to crumble into dust, disintegrating beneath the force of your resolve. The torment that whispered insidious lies is exiled, banished from the sacred space, where your healing now lives and breathes.

And as you release the burdens that once weighed so heavily upon you, something extraordinary occurs. *Light* does not merely arrive—it *consumes*. It surges in, breaking past walls long fortified by sorrow, flooding and illuminating even the most hidden corners of your being. It is not a flickering ember; it's wildfire, an untamed blaze.
It doesn't simply warm—*it ignites*.
It doesn't merely comfort—*it transforms*.

Within that Holy fire, the remnants of despair are burned away, reduced to ash—revealing the brilliance that lay beneath the ruins. You aren't merely free—you are reborn. You no longer carry the weight of what it was; you carry the light of what it is and the promise of what will be. Forgiveness isn't forgetting, it's *rising*. It's standing amidst the wreckage and declaring, with the unwavering conviction of a soul unbreakable:

I am radiant. I am whole. I am unstoppable.

You choose joy over torment, truth over accusation, and glory over ruin. The scars you once bore—etched deep as memorials of suffering—no longer carry the weight of agony. They've *transformed*. They gleam now—radiant and resplendent—not as wounds, but as *trophies of triumph,* shining proof that the battle didn't consume you... it refined you. Your story is no longer merely one of survival.

It's one of *redemption,* where loss gave birth to strength. It's one of *restoration,* where brokenness has given way to *wholeness*. It's one of divine healing, where what was shattered has been made Holy.

You now rise—not as the victim the world tried to define, but as the *Warrior* God ordained. You stand, crowned not by the weight of suffering, but by the *glory of resilience*. The hands that once trembled now wield *authority*. The voice that once faltered now speaks *life*. Today, you reclaim the narrative—not as a whisper, but as a *proclamation*. Today, you step forward—not cautiously, but *boldly*. You are *unbroken*. You are *undaunted*. You are *relentless*. And nothing—not the past, not the scars, not the voices that sought to silence you—can deny the *radiance* of what you have become.

Every trial, every storm, every crushing weight of suffering was never meant to destroy you—It was sent to *forge* you. It was the fire that *refined,* burning away doubt and fear, leaving only the brilliance of unshakable strength. It was the sculptor's chisel, shaping you—carving *endurance* into your soul, molding *resilience* into every fiber of your being. It was the divine hand, weaving *grace* though your wounds, transforming every scar into *sacred testimony.*

You aren't merely the *wounded,* defined by the pain that sought to silence you. You aren't merely the *abandoned,* left behind in the wake of betrayal. You aren't merely the victim the world tried to name you. No—You are more.

You are *glorious,* crowned with the radiance of redemption. You are *victorious,* walking in the triumph that suffering couldn't steal. You are *eternal,* anchored in a promise that transcends the fleeting shadows of struggle. You are an *Overcomer*—not because you escaped the fire, but because you endured it... and emerged transformed. You are a *living testament* to the power of God—an unshaken witness to His ability to turn mourning into joy, sorrow into strength, ashes into beauty.

You're not just a survivor—*you're a conqueror.*
You're not just restored—*you're resurrected.*
You're not just standing—*you're ascending.*

A beacon of divine triumph, shining with the untouchable light of grace, walking in the fullness of your calling—*bold, unbroken, unstoppable.* And nothing—*Nothing*—can dim the radiance of who you've become.

Your ministry stands before you—waiting, *beckoning*—to be embraced. Heaven itself leans forward in anticipation, watching as the mantle of divine purpose is laid upon your shoulders. This calling is not coincidence—it's *divinely orchestrated,* a summons that echoes through eternity.

Just as we have witnessed countless souls being filled with the Holy Ghost, baptized in *Jesus Name*, and transformed beyond human understanding—so too has God *called you.* The same Spirit that surged through the upper room, that shook the foundations of prisons, that parted seas and raised the dead—*that power now longs to dwell within you.* It moves through generations, resting upon those who are willing, and ignites purpose within those bold enough to believe.

But remember this: *God has never called the mighty—He has called the broken.* He has never chosen the strongest—He has chosen the least expected, the ones overlooked, the ones dismissed, the ones whose hands were empty, whose hearts were shattered. Because it's in *that very brokenness* that He performs His greatest miracles. It's in *that emptiness* that He pours out His fullness. It's in *that weakness* that His strength is made perfect.

We were the wounded, yet He made us whole. We were the abandoned, yet He called us *chosen.* We were the lost, yet He crowned us *redeemed*. And so too, will He do the same for *you*. You stand at the threshold of something greater than you ever imagined. Not by your own power, but by *His*. Not by your own wisdom, but by *His*. Not by your own strength, but by *His*. So, take hold of His Promise. *Step forward into your calling*; Heaven is waiting, and His Spirit is moving, and destiny is unfolding before you.

Healing isn't merely relief—it is *rebirth*. It's the sacred exchange where wounds are no longer chains but wings—where scars become testaments rather than burdens. The pain that once sought to *shatter you* becomes the platform from which you rise—*stronger, wiser, untouchable*.

Healing is the bridge, and wholeness is the destination—the final, undeniable declaration of *victory*. It's the moment when you're no longer shaped by what tried to destroy you, but by the *restoration* that followed. It's the bold reality of standing unshaken, walking in divine identity, pouring into others without depletion, and living with a heart unchained by fear.

Healing is the doorway to that wholeness. Without it, we drag the weight of unhealed wounds into every step we take—our past echoing into our future, our pain dictating our present. But when healing is *embraced*—when it's given space to transform rather than simply soothe—we are not merely restored—*we are remade*.

We don't simply return to who we were we transcend it. We don't simply recover we resurrect. We don't merely heal we become whole. And *wholeness*—true, unbreakable, undeniable wholeness—is the greatest victory of all.

Isaiah 61:3 unveils a breathtaking revelation of God's power to redeem and restore, proving that what was once lost is never beyond His reach. In His infinite grace, He does not simply lift us from the ruins—*He transforms them.* He breathes new life into the broken places, turning sorrow into joy, weaving despair into a tapestry of divine purpose. The ashes—once symbols of mourning and loss—become the very soil from which beauty blooms, a masterpiece sculpted by His loving hands. What was shattered is gathered. What was broken is refined and what was ruined is remade—evolving stronger, more radiant, more glorious than before.

We do not simply rise; we emerge—clothed in His mercy, crowned in His glory, *wholly restored.* Every tear, every trial, every shadow of pain isn't forgotten but woven into a narrative of wholeness—a testimony of faith refined in fire, bursting forth with a brilliance that could only be born of *redemption.*

In Him, *nothing is wasted.* No suffering is meaningless, no brokenness irredeemable. He takes the shattered fragments—the remnants of what once seemed beyond repair—and, like a Master Artisan, He crafts something breathtaking. What was ashes becomes a crown of beauty; what was despair becomes a song of triumph; what was lost is restored—*greater than before.* You're not merely restored—*you are reborn.* You're not merely lifted—*you are transformed.* You're not merely healed—*you are*

254

complete. And that *wholeness is your victory, your divine inheritance*, your *everlasting testimony.* You're God's masterpiece—*beauty rising from the ashes.*

Now stand, step forward—*not merely restored, but whole.* Walk in the fullness of His promises, carrying the divine imprint of redemption upon your life. The past no longer defines you; the pain no longer holds you. You are *living proof* that ashes do not mark the end—they mark the *beginning* of something *glorious.*

What once lay in ruins, has become *a temple of Honor and Grace.* What once was broken was made *whole.* And in the radiance of His presence, *you shine*—not dimly, not fleetingly, but *eternally*, as a vessel of His *magnificent grace.*

Healing is the divine embrace that lifts you from the depths of sorrow, carrying you into a realm where brokenness isn't just repaired—but reborn into something radiant. It's the whisper of God's Grace calling you out of darkness... a sacred threshold where burdens dissolve, wounds are touched by His hand, and the soul takes its first deep breath after years of struggle. Healing is the moment when despair loses its grip and hope takes root— when the shattered fragments of your past begin to realign beneath the weight of His loving restoration.

Yet healing is not the destination—it's the bridge to something greater. *Wholeness* is the masterpiece of redemption, the divine completion where scars cease to be marks of pain and transform into echoes of victory. In Him, wholeness isn't merely being mended—it's being made new, reimagined, and woven into the fullness of His love. It's a place where sorrow no longer lingers in the corners of your heart but becomes the foundation upon which joy is built.

To be healed is to rise, to be whole is to soar. Wholeness is where wounds no longer ache—they become gateways to wisdom, where brokenness is no longer a hindrance—but a testimony of triumph. It's the moment you step forward—not just restored but gloriously renewed, overflowing with His peace, dwelling in the abundance of His unshakable love.

In wholeness, you no longer search for purpose—*you become the embodiment of it.* You no longer wonder if you are enough—*you rest in the truth that in Him, you lack nothing.*

It's where survival transforms into *flourishing*—where the weight of the past no longer shackles but fuels the journey ahead. Wholeness is where redemption breathes life into every space that once knew sorrow—where grace overflows and where love—*pure, boundless, perfect*—becomes the essence of who you are. In Him, wholeness isn't just possible, *it's promised,* and it's yours to embrace.

Now, to *you—the seeker, the dreamer, the one standing on the precipice of change.* This moment is sacred, a threshold where the echoes of your past meet the promise of your future. You are on the brink of something profound—not just a shift in circumstance, but a *rebirth* of your very being.

Do not shrink from the unknown; *reach toward it.* Stretch beyond comfort, for within the divine unfolding of your journey, *transformation stirs.* You aren't merely enduring—*you are rising.* Let yourself be challenged, let yourself be uplifted, and above all, let yourself believe in the greatness that is already within you.

Beyond the horizon, *wholeness calls,* beckoning you toward the fullness of your purpose. Don't settle for *almost.* Don't hesitate at the edge of breakthrough. Press on—push through. Let *faith* drown out hesitation. Let *hope* roar louder than doubt. Let the voice of *Truth,* fierce and unwavering, silence every whisper that urges retreat.

This is your *awakening.* The veil of hesitation lifts, revealing the boundless horizon ahead. Step forward, unafraid, for destiny does not wait—*it beckons.* The future is yours to claim—shaped not by chance but by the courage you carry, the faith you embrace, and the unshakable belief that *you were made for more.*

Let the Holy Ghost ignite within you. Let conviction anchor you. Let boldness propel you beyond every limitation that once dared to hold you back. You are not merely stepping forward— *you are ascending.* Rise into your purpose, into your power, into the life that's been waiting for *you.*

No more hesitation. No more doubt. The threshold has been crossed, and now, there is only *becoming.*

Hear me: If no one has ever spoken these words into your heart, then *let them take root*, let them settle deep within your spirit: *I believe in you.* But more than that—*Jesus believes in you.* He doesn't just see you; *He beholds you*, not with scrutiny, but with the eyes of *perfect love.* He doesn't just know you—*He formed you*, every thread, woven with divine intention. And He doesn't just love you—*He loves you wholly, fiercely, unconditionally—without reservation.* His love isn't bound by your past. It doesn't falter your flaws, nor is it conditional, fleeting, or subject to the whims of the world. His love is eternal—an ocean without shores, a gift without price, poured out from the heart of the Almighty with unrelenting grace.

You don't have to earn it. You don't have to prove your worth. His love has already been written into the fabric of your existence, etched into the breath that fills your lungs—spoken over you before time itself called your name.

So, stand in it, rest in it, and let it carry you beyond doubt, beyond hesitation, beyond every whisper that has ever made you question your belonging.

You are loved, entirely, unwaveringly and fiercely.

And this journey—the pursuit of healing, of restoration, of divine wholeness—it is not a fragile hope or some distant dream to chase. It's a promise, spoken over you by the One who formed you with intention, who calls you by name, who has crafted every detail of your life with eternal purpose.

So, step boldly into the promise that stands before you—not with timid steps, not with cautious hesitation, but with a heart set ablaze by expectation. For the Author of your life isn't merely writing a story—He is crafting a masterpiece, a tapestry of redemption, where beauty is born from ashes, where light shatters the deepest shadows, where hope refuses to be extinguished.

Watch as grace, like the finest brushstroke, sweeps across the canvas of your existence. Every line, every shade, every intricate detail is guided by the hand of the Master Artist—the One who doesn't merely see your *broken pieces* but holds them with love, shaping them into something *breathtaking*. He sees beyond your scars, beyond your doubts, beyond the voices that whispered "not enough"—He calls you *beloved* and breathes *wholeness* into the depths of your soul.

Let His love be the canvas on which your future is painted— the foundation upon which your destiny stands unshaken. Let it burn within you like a *Holy Fire*—igniting your calling, stirring your spirit, propelling you forward with *unrelenting strength.* Let Him be the anchor that steadies your steps, the peace that silences every storm, the unshakable truth that drowns out the lies of fear and hesitation.

You aren't simply moving forward—you are stepping into Divine Fulfillment. The story is unfolding, the masterpiece is being revealed, and His love—His unshakable, unstoppable love—is the force that holds every fiber of it together.

As you walk, may each step be infused with the sacred breath of renewal—a symphony of redemption echoing through the corridors of your soul. May your healing be not a fleeting moment, but a *divine metamorphosis*—an unfolding of wholeness that rewrites your very existence with *grace, power, and purpose.*

For this isn't just healing—it's the *restoration* of all that was lost, the *reclamation* of all that was stolen, the *unveiling* of the masterpiece that has always been within you. It's redemption—the breaking of strongholds, the shattering of limitations, the awakening of glory. It is transformation—a rebirth into radiant strength, a rising into unshakable identity, a stepping into divine fullness. It's wholeness—the mending of every fractured place, the weaving together of what seemed irreparable, the *Holy completion* that stands unmovable. *Rise, walk, and step forward*—not as one merely surviving—but as one fully *alive,* fully *renewed*, fully made *whole.*

This—This is your Divine invitation to rise.

In the exalted Name of Jesus Christ of Nazareth—Rise up and walk.

Stand: Not as one merely hoping, but as one fully *assured.* Not only into promise, but into *fulfillment.* Not with hesitation, but with *sacred confidence.* Let fear dissolve, let doubt be silenced, let every lingering shadow flee in the presence of His light. *You are unshaken. You are unbound. You are well able...*

Rise: Shake off the weight of yesterday's sorrow, break free from the chains of uncertainty, stand victorious over the lies that once whispered against your destiny. Cast aside every hindrance, for you are held—wrapped securely in the unwavering embrace of *divine mercy* and *unbreakable love.*

Walk: Continue as one who has been wholly restored.
Walk under the Authority of Heaven…
In the Brilliance of Redemption…
In the Triumph of Divine Transformation…
Step into the fullness of who you were created to be—into the immeasurable richness of your calling, into the boundless depths of your Holy purpose.

Although these final words mark the end of this book, they do not mark the end of your journey.
This is your beginning—
A rising from the ashes,
A reclaiming of all that was lost,
A redemption of all that was once broken.

What was discarded has now been gathered. What was discouraged has now been strengthened. What once lay shattered has now been woven back together with divine hands—
Mended with grace,
Sealed with purpose.

You are *not* who you were before.
You are restored—

You are rebirthed—
You are whole.

So, step forward—Not into an ending, but into the *unfolding* of your sacred destiny.
This is your time…
This is your calling…
This is your divine invitation to walk boldly into the wholeness of who you were always meant to be…

Rise and never look back, you got this!

About The Author

Yvonne Rimmer is a passionate speaker, minister, and encourager with a heart for those journeying from brokenness to healing—and healing to wholeness. With unwavering compassion, she walks alongside souls wounded by abuse and trauma, offering not only hope but a pathway to restoration through the transformative power of Christ. Through raw personal testimony and profound Biblical truths, Yvonne uplifts, inspires, and equips others to embrace healing, step into wholeness, and live a life of Divine purpose and freedom.

Yvonne co-leads **God's Handywork Inc. Ministries**—an impactful ministry that touches lives across all generations. While Yvonne speaks to the deepest wounds with spiritual healing and encouragement, Tim ministers through humor, infusing joy and laughter into every message. Their combined approach creates a unique ministry experience, blending faith, laughter, creative lessons, Godly counsel, and heartfelt hope— making the love of Jesus both tangible and transformative. A devoted wife, mother of four, and grandmother to a growing number of cherished grandchildren, Yvonne's life is a living testament to God's boundless Grace and restorative power. She knows firsthand that no wound is too deep, no past too broken, and no heart too lost for His redeeming love. Her latest book, *Marie's Awakening*, continues the journey begun in *Marie's Journey*, furthering her mission to uplift, encourage, and equip others through the power of testimony and truth.

Connect with Me

I Would love to stay in touch with you.
If you'd like to follow along on my journey, here's where you can find me:

Website: www.godshandywork.org

Email: mawclown@bellsouth.net

Facebook: @yvonne.rimmer.5

www.ingramcontent.com/pod-product-compliance
Lightning Source LLC
Chambersburg PA
CBHW071630140626
46555CB00022B/2047